Analyzing interaction

Analyzing interaction:
Sequential analysis with
SDIS & GSEQ

ROGER BAKEMAN
Georgia State University

and

VICENÇ QUERA
University of Barcelona

CAMBRIDGE
UNIVERSITY PRESS

Published by the Press Syndicate of the University of Cambridge
The Pitt Building, Trumpington Street, Cambridge CB2 1RP
40 West 20th Street, New York, NY 10011-42111, USA
10 Stamford Road, Oakleigh, Melbourne 3166, Australia

First published 1995

Printed in the United States of America

Library of Congress Cataloging-in-Publication Data
Bakeman, Roger
Analyzing interaction : sequential analysis with SDIA & GSEQ /
Roger Bakeman and Vicenç Quera.
p.   cm.
Includes bibliographical references and index.
ISBN 0-521-44451-9 (hard). – ISBN 0-521-44901-4 (pbk.)
1. Social psychology – Methodology.   2. Sequential analysis –
Computer programs.   3. Social interaction – Statistical methods –
Computer programs.   I. Quera, Vicenç.   II. Title.
HM251.B245   1995
305′.01 – dc20   94-45280

A catalog record for this book is available from the British Library.

ISBN 0-521-44451-9 Hardback
ISBN 0-521-44901-4 Paperback

Contents

Preface

This book is the result of more than a decade of thinking about how to easily and efficiently analyze sequential observational data. If you collect such data, and have found general-purpose computer packages of little help and custom computer programs difficult and time consuming to develop, then you may find here the tools you have been seeking. Although you will need some knowledge of inferential and contingency table statistics, we think you will find the computer programs themselves relatively easy to use.

This book and its accompanying computer programs have roots in programs we wrote in the early 1980s. Long before we met, we had developed the programs ELAG (Bakeman, 1983) and ANSEC (Quera & Estany, 1984), both of which were designed to do lag sequential analysis. We each realized the limitations of these early programs and had begun designing successors. Then in 1991 we met, talked about our plans, and realized the many advantages of joining forces. The present volume is the result. We believe ours is the first software for sequential analysis that is easily adaptable to a diversity of data and research needs. And probably it is one of only a handful of programs designed to accommodate both English and Spanish speakers.

Many people – some known, some unknown – have helped us in our task. We owe a substantial intellectual debt to Gene Sackett, who essentially defined lag sequential analysis, and who early on encouraged our interest. And we certainly thank Jesús Palacios, who saw merit in sequential analysis, and invited one of us (RB) to speak at the University of Seville. But Maria Teresa Anguera, perhaps more than anyone else, has influenced and affected us both. She chairs the Departamento de Metodología de las Ciencias del Comportamiento (Psychology Faculty, University of Barcelona), served as VQ's mentor, and with Angel Blanco translated into Spanish RB's earlier book on observational methodology (Bakeman & Gottman, 1986). She also invited RB to speak at the University of Barcelona after his visit in Seville, and so made it inevitable that we would meet.

This work was greatly facilitated by all those unnamed visionaries who contributed to the development of the nets (bit-, inter-, and so forth). Perhaps this book would have been possible without the essentially instant passing back and forth of messages, text, and programs, but it is becoming increasingly difficult to remember how we managed in the era of letters, typewriters, and carbon paper.

Several colleagues and students have helped us by reading and commenting on the text and by checking out the programs. Robert Casey, José Manuel Juárez, and Donna Borkman Reed have been especially helpful, but we also owe thanks to Maribel Baldellou, Ana D'Ocón, Montse Balaguer, and Maria Dolors Girbau. In addition, RB thanks Daryl Nenstiel, and VQ thanks Esther Estany for their support and patience and their tolerance of the computers in their lives.

1

Applied sequential analysis: Basic tools and terms

Topics covered in this chapter include:

1. An introduction to the Sequential Data Interchange Standard (SDIS), which defines a standard format for sequential data.
2. An introduction to a Generalized Sequential Querier (GSEQ) computer program for manipulating, describing, and analyzing SDIS-formatted data.
3. The usefulness of log-linear analysis for additional analyses of sequential data.
4. The four types of sequential data defined by SDIS and discussed throughout this book.

The present volume, *Analyzing Interaction: Sequential Analysis with SDIS and GSEQ*, is intended as a companion volume for *Observing Interaction: An Introduction to Sequential Analysis* (Bakeman & Gottman, 1986). *Observing Interaction* explains how to conceptualize, code, record, organize, and analyze sequential data, but it does not provide extensive and detailed strategic advice nor does it provide the requisite computational tools. Unfortunately, investigators who turn to the standard statistical packages (e.g., BMDP, SAS, SPSS, and SYSTAT) looking for general-purpose programs for sequential analysis are usually disappointed.

Analyzing Interaction is intended to remedy this situation. First, a powerful and general standardized format for sequential data (SDIS) is introduced. Next, a general-purpose computer program (GSEQ) that allows readers to describe and analyze their own sequential data is described. It is designed to run on IBM-compatible microcomputers, and a diskette containing copies of GSEQ and other support programs is included with this book. In chapter 2, four paradigmatic examples of sequential studies are introduced, and they are then used throughout the rest of the book to illustrate SDIS and GSEQ. Along the way, considerable practical and strategic advice about applied sequential analysis is offered. Thus, whereas *Observing Interaction* provides a broad overview and a conceptual base for sequential analyses, *Analyzing Interaction* provides focused examples and the tools necessary to actually do the work.

1.1 SDIS: Standardizing sequential data

Standard statistical packages have served researchers extremely well. No wonder that investigators often turn to SPSS or SAS, for example, to look for sequential analysis programs. But why is it that the standard packages compute everything from cross tabulations and means to multivariate analyses of variance, but in general do not do sequential analysis? Why, with only a few, fairly limited exceptions (e.g., Bakeman, 1983; Quera & Estany, 1984), are more general-purpose sequential analysis programs not available?

We believe that sequential analysis has suffered because no common standard structure or convention exists for sequential data. In the absence of a recognized standard, most researchers have developed their own conventions and their own programs; usually such programs are so tailored to a particular laboratory's work that they are difficult for others to use. Nonetheless, in addition to Bakeman's (1983) and Quera & Estany's (1984) programs, several others have been developed for the analysis of sequential data and have been made available to interested researchers (see, e.g., Arundale, 1984; Deni, 1977; Dodd, Bakeman, Loeber, & Wilson, 1981; Gardner, 1990; Kienapple, 1987; Sackett, Holm, Crowley, & Henkins, 1979; Schlundt, 1982; Symons, Wright, & Moran, 1988; and Yoder & Tapp, 1990).

If there were a sequential data interchange standard – a standard way of representing sequential data – and if researchers adhered to this standard, then laboratories could more easily share data and programs. Moreover, if many laboratories used the same format for their sequential data, then it would be more attractive to write general-purpose computer programs for such data. Thus, a standard set of conventions for sequential data would greatly facilitate the use of sequential techniques and would make such techniques more accessible to interested researchers.

Exactly such a standard, which we call the Sequential Data Interchange Standard, or SDIS, is defined and demonstrated in this book. It represents, we believe, a real advance in sequential analysis and was first described in the journal *Behavior Research Methods, Instruments, and Computers* (Bakeman & Quera, 1992). Our intent was to develop natural and easy-to-use conventions. They are easy to learn and easy to use when entering data into computer files, they allow researchers to represent aspects of the data that are important to them, and they greatly facilitate analysis of the data, as you will see in subsequent chapters.

1.2 GSEQ: A generalized sequential querier

Two major computer programs are included with this book. One of them, the SDIS program, reads data and checks that they follow SDIS conventions. If they do, then a modified version of the data, one that facilitates subsequent computer processing, is created. The second program analyzes the data. It is a far more general and powerful program than Bakeman's (1983) ELAG, which analyzed only one relatively simple kind of sequential data. We call this new program the Generalized Sequential Querier, or GSEQ, because it is a general-purpose analysis program for sequential data. Like SDIS, it runs on IBM-compatible microcomputers in a DOS environment. It reads SDIS or modified SDIS data as input and produces a variety of sequential statistics as output.

Both SDIS and GSEQ are designed to be natural and easy to use. At the same time, GSEQ gives the user considerable control. As you will see in subsequent chapters, it is easy to lump some codes for analysis while ignoring others, to request simple and conditional frequencies and probabilities for lagged and unlagged behaviors, and to specify rules for lagging. For example, lagging may be relative to a particular event, either preceding, following, or co-occurring with a given behavior. Or lagging may be relative to time, occurring within a specified time of the onset or offset of a given event or time interval. If the preceding sentences did not make complete sense to you, do not worry. Their meaning, and usefulness, should become clear by the time you finish reading this book.

1.3 Basic statistics: From lags to logs

Sequential analysis is not a single unified statistical topic like the analysis of variance or multiple regression. Instead it is the application of a number of existing techniques to sequential categorical data. Nonetheless our understanding of which techniques are relevant and how they should be applied has developed dramatically during the past 20 years.

Early articles stressed the binomial test z score and lag-sequential analysis (e.g., Bakeman, 1978; Bakeman & Dabbs, 1976; Sackett, 1979). Allison and Liker (1982) agreed that a z score could be used to test sequential dependency, but noted that the binomial computation recommended in the early articles was technically incorrect and that a slightly different computation should be used instead (because expected cell frequencies were estimated from the marginals, not determined a priori; see Bakeman & Gottman, 1986). They also suggested that log-linear modeling might be used but did not develop that idea in any detail.

Observational data of the sort appropriate for sequential analyses can almost always be summarized in the form of multidimensional contingency tables. Castellan (1979) may have been the first to point this out and, as just noted, Allison and Liker (1982) explicitly suggested log-linear techniques (which analyze multidimensional contingency tables) in their much-cited paper. Yet for much of the 1980s researchers interested in sequential analysis rarely used log-linear analyses (exceptions are Cohn & Tronick, 1987; and Stevenson, Ver Hoeve, Roach, & Leavitt, 1986), even though such analyses are probably among the most appropriate ones for sequential data (see, e.g., Bakeman, 1991; Bakeman, Adamson, & Strisik, 1989; Budescu, 1984; Gottman & Roy, 1990; Iacobucci & Wasserman, 1988; cf. Faraone & Dorfman, 1987).

GSEQ, the general sequential analyzing program included with this book, is best understood as a powerful descriptive tool. It allows you to define two-dimensional tables in remarkably flexible ways, and then scans the data, tabulating counts for the tables you have defined. It also computes a number of useful and informative statistics for each two-dimensional table. After exhausting the descriptive potential of GSEQ, some users will want to move on to subsequent analyses of multidimensional tables formed by combining several of GSEQ'S two-dimensional tables. This is easy to do. The standard statistical packages include quite usable log-linear programs (e.g., LOGLINEAR and HILOGLINEAR in SPSS) and, in addition, Bakeman and Robinson (1994) have written an interactive microcomputer program called ILOG specifically for log-linear analysis. When requested, GSEQ produces output that can be passed more or less directly to such programs.

1.4 Sequential data: Events, states, times, and intervals

Sequential data can result from coding specified successive events or successive time intervals. Nothing more than the order of events, or the occurrence or non-occurrence of events within specified time intervals, might be recorded. Or recording might preserve the onset times for some events and onset and offset times for others. There are other more complex possibilities as well, but, partly to ease exposition and partly to facilitate preparation of data for analysis, we have found it convenient to have SDIS recognize four basic categories or types of sequential data:

1. ESD, or Event Sequential Data
2. SSD, or State Sequential Data (including MSD, or Multiple State Data)
3. TSD, or Timed Event Sequential Data
4. ISD, or Interval Sequential Data

The first (ESD) preserves a record of events only. For example,

> A B C

indicates that event A was followed by B, which in turn was followed by C. The second (SSD) preserves time or duration information as well. For example,

> A,10:30 B,10:42

indicates that state A started at 10:30 and state B started at 10:42 (thus state A continued up to 10:42), whereas

> A,10:30 B,10:42 & X,10:30 Y,10:36

indicates that a second stream co-occurred with the first (MSD); in this case both began at 10:30. The third type (TSD) allows for both momentary and duration events, which may overlap. For example,

> A,10:30-10:42 B,10:33 C,10:37-10:54 B,10:50

indicates that event A started at 10:30 and continued up to 10:42, event C started at 10:37 and continued up to 10:54, and event B occurred at 10:33 and again at 10:50. Finally, the fourth type (ISD) imposes its own time-interval metric on the passing stream of behavior. For example,

> A B, A, B C D

indicates that events A and B occurred during the first interval; event A occurred during the second interval; and events B, C, and D occurred during the third interval.

The first three data types are alike in that for each of them recording is activated by the events that occur (although time is recorded only for SSD and TSD, not ESD), whereas recording for interval sequences (ISD) is activated by time, usually the end of an interval. In the following paragraphs we define each of these data types in more detail and describe how they differ from definitions given in *Observing Interaction*. Then in chapter 2 we describe studies that exemplify each of the four data types, and in chapters 3 and 4 we provide formal definitions and further exam-

Table 1.1. *Characteristics of data types recognized by SDIS and GSEQ.*

Characteristic	Data Type				
	Event (ESD)	State (SSD)	Multiple State (MSD)	Timed Event (TSD)	Interval (ISD)
Do events activate recording?	Yes	Yes	Yes	Yes	No
Are onset times recorded?	No	Yes	Yes	Yes	No
Can codes co-occur?	No	No	Yes	Yes	Yes
Are offset times recorded as well?	No	No	No	Yes	No
Is recording tied to time intervals?	No	No	No	No	Yes

ples. Some of the differences among these data types are summarized in Table 1.1.

Event sequences

Event sequences consist simply of coded events. Duration of individual events is not of interest. By definition, event sequential data consist of a single stream of coded events without any sort of time information for the individual events. Thus the coded events are necessarily mutually exclusive; only one can occur at a time. Sometimes, depending on the nature of the codes, two identical codes can follow themselves in the stream (e.g., A B A A B B B). Events may be observed live or on video-tape, but because the form is so simple, recording often requires nothing more elaborate than pencil and paper.

State Sequences

After event sequences, state sequences are probably the simplest of the four data types defined here. State sequences consist of one or more streams of coded events or states recorded in a way that preserves time information for each state. In its simplest form, only one stream is recorded. The duration of individual states, and perhaps the co-occurrence of states in different streams, is usually of interest. The states within each stream or set are defined to be mutually exclusive and exhaustive; hence the beginning of a new state necessarily implies the end of the previous one. As we define matters, a single stream of states is like an event sequence to which time information has been added. Sometimes codes are not allowed to follow themselves within a stream, but whether adjacent codes are repeatable depends on the behavior coded; it is not part of our definition of a state sequence. Recording requires some sort of timing device, which could be a clock, a stopwatch, or a clock internal to a videorecorder that records the time directly on the videotape.

Timed event sequences

Timed event sequences allow for more complexity than event or state sequences. This is probably the most general of the four data types defined here. Codes may represent momentary or *frequency behaviors*, in which case only onset times need be recorded, or codes may represent *duration behaviors*, in which case both onset and offset times would be preserved. Events need not be mutually exclusive; indeed, often the co-occurrence of various events is of interest to the investigator. As we define matters, both single and multiple streams of state sequences could be represented as timed event sequences, but, as you will see later, there are advantages to preserving state sequences as a separate data type. Usually procedures for recording timed event sequences require electronic assistance, for example, videorecorders that can record the time on the videotape or microcomputers or similar recording devices with internal clocks.

Interval sequences

Interval sequences consist of a series of successive time intervals to which codes may be assigned. One or more codes may be allowed per interval and the time interval may be quite short, for example, only 5 or 10 seconds. Procedures that yield interval sequences are typically inexpensive and reliable (pencil, paper, and stopwatch) but do not always provide the most accurate information; hence this data type is often used when only approximate time information is desired and more accurate recording procedures are not feasible.

Interval recording methods are quite common in the literature but are becoming less so with the advent of modern electronic equipment. It seems likely that many investigators who used interval sequences in the past would have preferred the greater accuracy provided by timed event sequences, but only recently has recording the onsets and offsets of frequency and duration behaviors become relatively inexpensive and easy to do.

Earlier definitions

This section is provided for readers of *Observing Interaction* as an aid to translating definitions provided earlier. Bakeman and Gottman (1986) also defined four ways of representing sequential data, but their definitions differed somewhat from those used here. They used the term *event sequences* in essentially the same sense (although they suggested that in event sequences adjacent codes could not repeat, whereas here both possibilities are permitted). But they used the term *time sequences* to refer to both state sequences and interval sequences when only one code was permitted per interval.

The third term they used was *time-frame data*, which included what we now call multiple-stream state data, timed event data, and interval data (when more than one code is permitted per interval). Thus in Bakeman and Gottman's (1986) earlier usage, event and time sequences referred to streams of coded events or intervals that did not permit co-occurrences, whereas time-frame data did. Now we view time-frame data as an earlier attempt to define a standard format for complex sequential data, but think our current definitions provide more flexibility and agree more with what investigators do.

Cross-classified events was the fourth term used by Bakeman and Gottman (1986). Not an inherently sequential strategy, it refers to the multidimensional contingency tables that result from classifying events on several dimensions, each of which is represented with several codes or levels. Here we do not include multidimensional contingency tables as one of the four basic types of sequential data. Instead, we recognize that multidimensional contingency tables often result from GSEQ analysis of sequential data, and may be subjected to log-linear analyses later.

1.5 Summary

Some basic terms and tools (see Table 1.2) for sequential analysis have been presented in this chapter and we have explained how this book both complements and extends its companion volume, *Observing Interaction*. In particular, four data types – event, state, timed event, and interval sequences – were introduced, which, we believe, can be used to represent most sequential data we have encountered. In the next chapter, four paradigmatic studies are described, each exemplifying a different data type. These studies are then used in subsequent chapters to demonstrate sequential analysis generally and the features of SDIS and GSEQ in particular.

Table 1.2. *Terms introduced in chapter 1.*

Term	Mnemonic
Sequential Data Interchange Standard	SDIS
Generalized Sequential Querier	GSEQ
Event Sequential Data	ESD
State Sequential Data	SSD
Multiple State Data	MSD
Timed Event Sequential Data	TSD
Interval Sequential Data	ISD
Log-linear Analysis	–
Frequency (or Momentary) Behaviors	–
Duration Behaviors	–

2

Sequential examples: Talk, attention, distress, and infants

The four studies described in this chapter are:

1. The marital talk study, which exemplifies event sequential data.
2. The joint attention study, which exemplifies state sequential data.
3. The child distress study, which exemplifies timed event sequential data.
4. The !Kung infants study, which exemplifies interval sequential data.

Each study exemplifies a different type of sequential data and provides examples for the discussions of sequential data formats and sequential analysis occurring in subsequent chapters. These four paradigmatic studies are based on actual studies but have been simplified here for ease of exposition. Reading about them should give you a better sense of the four SDIS data types and their comparative advantages and uses.

2.1 Event sequences: Marital talk study

The marital talk study is inspired by many investigations of marital interaction and is based on a coding system first defined by Hops and his colleagues (Hops, Willis, Weiss, & Patterson, 1972). Imagine that couples recruited for a study of marital satisfaction are categorized as distressed or nondistressed. All couples are asked to list topics that cause tension between them and are then asked to discuss one of those problem topics. Their conversation is audiotaped or videotaped and transcripts of their conversation are prepared subsequently.

Coders, who are unaware of the couples' status (distressed versus nondistressed), read the transcripts (or attend to the tapes) and code each speaker's turn of talk using the following scheme:

1. Complains
2. Emotes
3. Approves

4. Empathizes
5. Negates
6. Other

These codes are mutually exclusive (only one code applies to each turn) and exhaustive (one of the codes applies to each turn).

Coded versions of each couple's discussion are then prepared. These note the couple involved, their status (distressed versus nondistressed), any other identifying or background information, and a list of the codes assigned to each successive turn of talk along with the speaker for that turn. The codes might be noted in the data files using either numbers (e.g., 4 = empathizes) or mnemonic abbreviations (e.g., EMP = empathizes). The identity of the speaker might be noted with an additional digit (e.g., 15 = husband negates or 25 = wife negates) or, again, mnemonic abbreviations might be used (e.g., HCom = husband complains or WCom = wife complains).

If mnemonics were used, a few lines of the SDIS data file might look like this:

> Event;
> % Event Sequential Data, Example File %
> <first couple>
> WEmp HNeg WCom HAp WCom HCom WEmo /
> <second couple>
> WEmp HCom WEmo HNeg WCom HAp WCom /

For now, do not worry about the punctuation and conventions used. These will be described in detail in chapters 3 and 4.

A variety of questions might be of interest and could be answered with these data, such as: Do distressed couples complain more than non-distressed couples? Are husbands more negative than wives? Do husbands respond to their wives' complaints with other complaints (called cross-complaining)? Do wives do the same? Is the tendency to answer one complaint with another confined primarily to distressed couples? Similarly, are nondistressed more likely than distressed couples to answer a complaint with empathizing?

Event sequences, such as those that would result from the marital talk study, constitute the simplest type of sequential data defined here. The data consist of a sequence of codes representing successive events, nothing more. No information concerning onset times or durations for the particular events is included. Such data are actually quite common. For example, when conversations of almost any kind are coded, event sequences usually result.

2.2 State sequences: Joint attention study

The joint attention study is based on research conducted by Adamson and Bakeman (e.g., Adamson & Bakeman, 1984; Bakeman & Adamson, 1984), which sought to document the development of joint attention in infants interacting with different partners. Imagine that infants are video-taped in their homes playing either with their mothers, with a peer, or alone for 10 minutes each and that videorecordings are made when the infants are 9, 12, and 15 months of age (in the actual study, 6- and 18-month old infants were also observed). Subsequently, coders segment the videotapes, which display time to the nearest second, into a series of *attentional states*. These states categorize the focus of the infant's attention as follows:

1. Unengaged: Infant not attending.
2. Onlooking: Infant observing another's actions, but not actively taking part.
3. Person: Infant engaged in face-to-face play with a person, but no objects are involved.
4. Object: Infant involved with objects, but no persons are involved.
5. Joint: Infant jointly engaged, that is, sharing attention to an object with another person.

As in the case for the codes used for the marital talk study, these codes are also mutually exclusive and exhaustive (ME&E).

The data coded from each of the 10-minute videotaped sessions note the infant involved; the partner (mother, peer, alone); the age of the infant at the time of videotaping; and the sequence and timing of attentional states. The states might be represented in the data file using numbers (e.g., 3 = person) or mnemonic abbreviations (e.g., Un, On, Pe, Ob, Jt). The engagement states characterize infants only, hence there is no need to indicate the actor – we know it is the infant, whereas for the marital talk study it was necessary to identify the speaker. However, in contrast to the marital talk data, which included no timing information, such information (either onset times or durations for the individual states) is included in state sequential data.

If mnemonics were used, the beginning of the SDIS data file might look like this:

```
State ( Un On Pe Ob Jt ) ;
% State Sequential Data, Example File %
<infant 026>
Un=2 Pe=3 Ob=1 Un=4 On=1 Ob=2 Un=5 /
```

Here, the observation session began with the infant unoccupied, which lasted for two time units. Then the infant switched to person engagement, which lasted for three time units, and so forth. Again, do not worry about the punctuation; exact conventions are detailed in chapters 3 and 4.

Questions that might motivate this study include: Are states (or episodes, or bouts) of joint engagement more frequent at some ages than others? Are they more frequent with some partners than others? Does the time spent in joint engagement, and other states as well, change with the infant's age? What typically follows an unengaged state? What typically precedes joint engagement? For example, is it more often object play or person play? Is the typical precursor for joint engagement different at different ages and with different partners?

As we define matters, state sequences are somewhat more complex than event sequences. For state sequences, coders record not just the sequence of events or states, but the times for each state as well (either durations or onset times from which durations can be derived). The word *state* is sometimes used to imply an underlying neural organization (as with infants' states such as alert or asleep). Here no such assumption is made. Later on we will complicate matters a bit, but for now it is sufficient to think of states as a sequence of (mutually exclusive and exhaustively defined) events whose duration in time is known.

2.3 Timed event sequences: Child distress study

The child distress study is based on research conducted by Manne and her colleagues (Manne, Bakeman, Jacobsen, Gorfinkle, Bernstein, & Redd, 1992) and is concerned with the effect of adults' behavior on children's distress during painful medical procedures. Imagine that children are videotaped during a venipuncture procedure that is part of the children's treatment for cancer. For purposes of analysis, the time during the procedure is broken down into three phases: preparation (child prepared for the procedure); insertion (vein located, needle inserted); and completion (blood drawn, therapy administered).

Trained observers view the videotapes, which display the time accurate to the nearest second. Some behaviors typically last only a few seconds and for these we want to know only when and how often they occurred, and so it is not necessary to record offset times. Other behaviors usually last longer, and for them we want to know duration as well. Accordingly, observers record just onset times for frequency or *momentary behaviors*, but both onset and offset times for *duration behaviors*. The coding scheme includes the following codes (the duration behaviors are noted; all others are momentary behaviors):

1. Child copes (duration)
2. Child evidences momentary distress
3. Child cries (duration)
4. Adult explains procedure to child (duration)
5. Adult distracts child (duration)
6. Adult gives control to child
7. Adult praises child

These codes are not mutually exclusive. In fact, which codes co-occur and the extent of their co-occurrence are often of considerable interest.

The data coded for each session note the child involved, the phase of the procedure, and the timing of the behaviors observed during that phase. Onset times for all codes would be recorded and offset times for the duration behaviors would be recorded as well. As with the other coding schemes, the actual codes entered in the data might be numeric (e.g., 11 = child copes, 21 = adult explains); alphabetic (e.g., Cope, Dtrs, Cry, Exp, Drct, GCon, Pras); or even alphanumeric (e.g., C1 = child copes, A1 = adult explains).

Again using mnemonic codes, the beginning of the SDIS data file might look like this:

> Timed;
> % Timed Event Sequential Data, Example File %
> <child A32>
> ,5:51 Dtrs,5:52 Exp,5:53-5:55 Cry,5:54-5:59 . . .

which indicates that the session began at 5:51. The child was momentarily distressed at 5:52, the adult explained from 5:53 up to 5:55, the child cried from 5:54 up to 5:59, and so forth.

Questions that data like these could answer include: If adults explain more during preparation, do children evidence less momentary distress during needle insertion? How do adults typically react to children's crying? Are there different types of reactions during different phases of the procedure? Are children more likely to begin coping just after adults have given them control or after adults have praised them? Is distraction an effective way to stop crying?

Timed event sequences are not as constrained as either event or state sequences and so more real-life complexity can be captured in the data. Codes may represent either momentary or duration behaviors and, because they need not be mutually exclusive and exhaustive, co-occurrences are easily represented. A single onset time indicates a momentary behavior, whereas a duration behavior is represented with a pair of onset and offset times. With TSD the investigator can determine not only how often momentary behaviors occur and what proportion of the time duration behaviors occur, but also whether some behaviors are more likely to begin just after (or just before) other behaviors have begun, or just before (or just after) other behaviors have ended. Thus timed event sequences allow for the investigation of temporal relations among behaviors (Did the infant stop crying within 5 seconds after the mother started rocking?) in a way that event and a single stream of state sequences do not.

2.4 Interval sequences: !Kung infants study

The !Kung infants study is based on Konner's study of !Kung infants' development and their interaction with others (Konner, 1976, 1977) and on recent reanalyses of Konner's data (Bakeman, Adamson, Konner, & Barr, 1990). Detailed records of the behavior of !Kung infants, and of others' reactions to them, were made by Konner in northwestern Botswana between 1969 and 1975. Konner observed !Kung infants at different ages using a detailed coding scheme that he had devised. Usually an infant at a particular age was observed for six 15-minute sessions, randomly distributed over the waking hours and completed within one week.

Konner recorded codable behaviors as they occurred on a lined recording form, letting each line represent five seconds. An electronic beeper delivered a signal every five seconds to an earpiece Konner wore, and so he knew when to move on to the next line. This resulted in interval sequences: a record of which codes occurred during each successive 5-second interval of the 15-minute recording session. (Electronic recording gear is not always the instrument of choice. Especially in remote locations, pencil and paper have much to offer; for example, as noted in *Observing Interaction*, they rarely malfunction.)

Konner's code catalog contained more than 100 codes, some of which rarely occurred. For the present example, imagine that only the following eight codes were defined (some of which result from lumping several of Konner's codes together):

1. Infant offers objects
2. Infant plays with object
3. Infant smiles or laughs
4. Infant vocalizes
5. Other offers objects to infant
6. Other encourages infant
7. Other entertains infant
8. Other vocalizes to infant

As was the case for the codes used for timed event sequences, these codes are not mutually exclusive and exhaustive.

The files for these interval sequences would note the usual session information (e.g., the particular infant observed and the infant's age), along with the codes checked for each successive interval. Again, the codes entered could be numeric (e.g., 1 = infant offers objects); alphabetic (IOfr, IObj, ISmi, IVoc, XOfr, XEnc, XEnt, XVoc); or alphanumeric (e.g., I1 = infant offers, X1 = other offers). The interval used for recording imposes a time structure on the data, thus no specific time information need be entered. Interval boundaries, however, do need to be indicated in some way.

Again using mnemonic codes, the beginning of the SDIS data file might look like this:

```
% Interval Sequential Data, Example File %
Interval=5;
<infant 52, 6mo>
,IVoc XEnt *2, XOfr, IOfr IVoc ISmi, . . .
```

which indicates that, in this case, intervals represent 5 time units. No behavior was coded for the first interval (no codes appear before the first comma), infant vocalizes and other entertains were coded for the next two intervals, infant offers for the following interval, infant offers and vocalizes and smiles for the interval after that, and so forth.

For those interested in the socialization of infants' early interest in objects, a number of questions arise, such as: At what age do !Kung infants begin spending time playing with objects? At what age do they begin offering objects? When infants play with objects do others encourage them? Vocalize to them? When infants smile and laugh and vocalize, what else are they doing? What are the others doing with them? When others offer infants objects, do the infants reciprocate?

Like timed event sequences, interval sequences are capable of capturing more complexity and allow for more subtle investigation of temporal relations than either event or single-stream state sequences. The resolution of interval sequences (i.e., the fineness of detail), however, is almost always more crude than that of timed event sequences.

The resolution for timed event sequences is limited by the timing device. Still, even though the clocks used are often accurate to the nearest second or better, it is fairly common to record times to the nearest second even when, for example, the videotapes being coded display time accurate to some fraction of a second. For the sorts of codes exemplified here, and taking human reaction time into account, accuracy to the nearest second usually seems more than sufficient. Greater accuracy may not be warranted. Moreover, such accuracy may require more memory and processing time, as discussed in chapter 3.

In contrast, the resolution of interval sequences is limited by the recording interval used, which almost always is considerably greater than the resolution of the timing device. For example, the interval for the !Kung infants study was 5 seconds. As a result, summary statistics derived from interval sequences will be somewhat biased compared to similar statistics derived from timed event sequences.

Researchers have long recognized these biases (for an excellent summary, see Suen & Ary, 1989) and have understood that interval recording is a compromise with the ideal. In fact, the merits of interval recording are all practical. It is inexpensive and reliable, and as a result interval recording has been widely used, especially before electronic recording devices and video equipment became as trustworthy and inexpensive as they are now. It is a simple trade-off. Recording interval sequences requires minimal expense and presents few technical problems, but offers less accurate and somewhat biased results. Recording timed event sequences, on the other hand, requires greater expense and equipment maintenance, but offers more accurate and sometimes immediately machine-readable results.

2.5 Summary

Four paradigmatic studies have been presented in this chapter (see Table 2.1). The marital talk study exemplifies event sequential data, the joint attention study exemplifies state sequential data, the child distress study exemplifies timed event sequential data, and the !Kung infants study exemplifies interval sequential data. These examples are based on actual studies but have been simplified somewhat for use in this book.

None of these studies exhausts the full range of ways researchers might collect sequential data. The recording of interval sequences, in particular, has spawned a technical literature, only some of which is hinted at here (but see chapter 4 and also Suen & Ary, 1989). Nonethe-

Table 2.1. *Studies introduced in chapter 2.*

Study	Type of Data
Marital Talk Study	Event Sequential Data
Joint Attention Study	State Sequential Data
Child Distress Study	Timed Event Sequential Data
!Kung Infants Study	Interval Sequential Data

less, these four studies provide clear and concrete examples of the four data types defined by SDIS and of the differences among them. They also provide a realistic context and a rich source of examples for subsequent discussions of SDIS and GSEQ. The next two chapters demonstrate specifically how data from these studies would be expressed using SDIS conventions.

3

Basic SDIS: Sessions,
conditions, times, and events

Topics covered in this chapter include:
1. How to signify the type of data in a file and how to form the behavioral codes in it.
2. How to organize codes by sessions, subjects, and conditions.
3. How to enter identifying information in the data file.
4. How to represent time using both decimal and sexagesimal conventions.
5. Syntax for session start and stop times.

This chapter and the next present the conventions used by SDIS, which were first published in *Behavior Research Methods, Instruments, and Computers* (Bakeman & Quera, 1992). The material presented in this chapter applies to all four data types and is sufficient to form event sequential data files. Further conventions, required for state, timed event, and interval sequential data, are presented in chapter 4.

3.1 SDIS data files

Files that contain event, state, timed event, or interval sequences, expressed according to SDIS conventions, are called SDIS data files and are standard ASCII files. An ASCII file is any file whose characters follow the American Standard Code for Information Interchange. Most simple text editors produce ASCII files, and more complex programs, such as word processors and spreadsheets, almost always have a way of producing ASCII files, although they may be called text or data files.

An SDIS data file consists of as many lines (sometimes called records in computer jargon) as are necessary. Information may be entered anywhere on a line; there are no fixed columns. Elements of the SDIS data language are separated by special characters (e.g., commas, semicolons, and other punctuation marks) and/or by one or more blanks, tabs, or returns (the end of line generated by the enter key). In theory, there is no limit to the length of a line, but in practice lines limited to a width that is easily displayed or printed are strongly recommended.

SDIS data files are processed by the SDIS program, which needs to know at the outset what type of data are in the file. Thus the first element in an SDIS data file is always a *type declaration*, which is either Event, State, Timed, or Interval. Type declarations are not case sensitive so, for example, EVENT or event could also be used. Single character abbreviations (i.e., E, S, T, or I) are also permitted.

The required type declaration may be followed by information about codes, as described in the next section, but in any case must be terminated with a semicolon to separate it from the data. The rest of the file contains coded data of the designated type, formatted and structured as described in this chapter and the next.

The overall structure of an SDIS data file is straightforward, and looks something like this:

> *Type*;
> <subject 1>
> . . . *data stream for subject 1* . . . */*
> <subject 2>
> . . . *data stream for subject 2* . . . */*
> . . .

The first line indicates the data type (Event, State, Timed, or Interval). Subsequent lines detail the data for the various subjects, beginning with identifying information enclosed in less-than and greater-than signs (optional) and followed by a terminating slash (required). These and other conventions are detailed throughout this chapter and the next.

When no errors are found, the SDIS program creates a new file called a modified SDIS, or MDS, file. This file contains essentially the same information as the original SDIS file, but is specially formatted so that GSEQ can process it efficiently.

3.2 Behavioral codes

Codes constitute the bulk of most SDIS data files and represent particular behaviors or events. They are formed from numbers, letters, or special characters, alone or in combination. Examples are

> 24 A WCom Jnt Cry X6 IVoc MOM_20 G_misc

Some special characters, specifically

> @ $ % & * ( ) = / - + : ; , .

have particular meanings in SDIS or GSEQ and may not be used, but others, specifically

> ! # ^ _ [ ] ?

may appear in code names. For example, you might use the underscore to separate actor and act identifiers (e.g., MOM_32, KID_D6). Typically it is convenient to use relatively short names for codes. We recommend using no more than 7 characters (although SDIS permits as many as 16) because GSEQ displays only the first 7 characters of a code's name. By default, uppercase and lowercase letters are not treated the same, thus CRY is not the same code as Cry or cry (i.e., code names are *case sensitive*). You may, however, instruct the SDIS program to ignore case (by setting the SDIS case sensitivity option to no; see chapter 9). This renders codes case insensitive, in which case CRY and cry would be regarded as the same code.

Declared codes

By default, the SDIS program creates a list of all codes encountered in the SDIS data file. This is convenient, but it means that if Pras were intended, Pars (or PRas, or pras, assuming case sensitivity) would be regarded as a new code instead of a data entry error. If you wish, you may provide SDIS with a list of all legitimate codes instead. This list is entered just after the type declaration (Event, State, etc.) that begins the SDIS data file and before its terminating semicolon. For example, the data file for the child distress study might begin with

> Timed Cope Dtrs Cry Exp Drct GCon Pras; . . .

in which case any code encountered subsequently in the data file that was not on this list would be flagged as an error. Codes in this list may be separated with either blanks or commas. However, in the data proper, only blanks separate codes; commas either demarcate intervals or indicate that a time (session start or stop time, code onset or offset time) follows.

Most of the time you will probably want to list explicitly the codes allowed. Not only are erroneous codes flagged, but GSEQ then displays codes in the order you provide. Otherwise, GSEQ would display codes in the order they are first encountered in the SDIS file. In any case, the number of unique codes either declared explicitly or appearing in the file may not exceed 95, a value we think should easily accommodate most researchers' needs.

Mutually exclusive and exhaustive sets of declared codes

Declared codes that constitute a mutually exclusive and exhaustive (ME&E) set may be enclosed in parentheses. Then SDIS, GSEQ, and other subsequent analysis programs can use this information. For example, if two codes are declared ME&E and yet overlap in a timed event data file, then SDIS will note the error. If you do not want codes checked for mutual exclusivity, checking can be turned off (by setting the SDIS exclusivity check option to no; see chapter 9).

Sets of mutually exclusive and exhaustive codes can be named. Set names begin with a dollar sign and are followed by an equals sign, thus

State ($IState= Cry Sleep Alert)
($Position= Supine 45_Degree Upright);

defines two sets of ME&E codes, one for an infant's state and one for position. One further example: in an event sequential data file all codes are ME&E by definition. Thus all codes could be enclosed in parentheses, or subsets could be defined and named. For example, using codes from the marital talk study,

Event ($Wife = WCom WEmo WAp WEmp WNeg WOth)
($Husband = HCom HEmo HAp HEmp HNeg HOth);

defines a set of wife codes and a set of husband codes. Each set has a name and so instead of listing all six husband codes or all six wife codes on a subsequent GSEQ command, the set name could be used instead.

If you enclose sets of codes in parentheses, and do not provide a name for the set, SDIS provides one automatically. The default name is Set_1 for the first set, Set_2 for the second, and so forth. Thus if you provided explicit names for the first and third sets, the default name for the second would be Set_2. In addition, code names not enclosed in parentheses are assigned the set name NO_SET by default. Either explicit or default names may be used in subsequent GSEQ commands.

Code names need not be enclosed in parentheses, of course – only those that form ME&E sets. But if any codes are listed after the Event, State, Timed, or Interval declaration, whether parts of sets or not, then those codes and only those codes will be permitted in the data that follow.

3.3 Sessions, subjects, and conditions

A *session* consists of a sequence of coded events for which continuity can be assumed. At a minimum, every SDIS file contains data for at least one session. If data were collected for only one session from only one subject, then the SDIS data file would look like this:

> *Type*;
> *. . . data for session 1, subject 1 . . . /*

As you can see, the data stream for a subject is terminated with a slash. Sometimes, however, a subject is observed for several sessions. In that case, earlier sessions are terminated with semicolons. For example,

> WEmp HNeg WCom HAp WCom HCom WEmo;

and

> 24 15 21 13 21 11 22;

represent brief sessions as might appear in an event sequential data file. They would be followed by other sessions for the same subject, and a slash would terminate the last session.

Sessions may be planned, or separate sessions may result from unplanned breaks during observation (e.g., an outside event intruding). In any event, it is important to represent sessions faithfully because GSEQ accumulates lagged statistics within sessions but not across session breaks.

Subjects

Every SDIS file contains data for at least one subject. As just noted, a *subject* could be observed for a single session or for several separate sessions, as the !Kung infants were. In that case a segment of the data might look as follows:

> *session; session; session; session; session; session/*

which represents data for a subject in the !Kung infant study who was observed for six sessions. Similarly,

> *session; session/ session; session; session/ session; session/*

represents observations for three subjects from the joint attention study. The first and third subjects were observed for two sessions whereas the second subject was observed for three sessions, presumably because some event (like baby becoming severely upset or the doorbell ringing) caused a break in the videotaping. Note that we use the term *subject* generically; it could refer to an individual person, an animal, a couple, a family, an infant at a particular age, and so forth.

Conditions

Optionally, subjects may be assigned to *conditions* as defined by a single or multiple factor design. This allows GSEQ to accumulate tallies and report statistics separately for the different cells of the design. If present, design information is enclosed in left and right parentheses and entered before the slash that terminates a subject's data. For example,

> *. . . data stream for subject 1 . . .* (1)/
> *. . . data stream for subject 2 . . .* (1)/
> *. . . data stream for subject 3 . . .* (2)/

indicates that subjects 1 and 2 belong to group 1, whereas subject 3 belongs to group 2.

It is not necessary to enter design information for every subject. If all subjects who occupy the same cell in a design are grouped together, then design information need be entered for the last subject only. For example,

> *session/ session/ session* (1)/
> *session/ session/ session* (2)/

represents data for six subjects from the marital talk study. The first three were from the distressed group (group 1) and the second three were from the nondistressed group (group 2); only one session was coded for each subject. Similarly,

> *session/ session; session* (1,1)/
> *session/ session* (1,2)/
> *session* (2,3)/
> *session/ session; session/ session* (3,3)/

represents data for eight infants from the joint attention study. The first number in parentheses indicates the partner (1 = mother, 2 = peer, 3 = alone), and the second indicates age (1 = 9, 2 = 12, 3 = 15 months). The first two infants were observed with their mothers at 9 months (condition 1,1); the third and fourth infants were observed with their mothers at 12 months (1,2); the fifth was observed with a peer at 15 months (2,3); and the sixth through eighth were observed alone at 15 months (3,3). One session was coded for some subjects, two for others.

It is important to understand that session refers to an uninterrupted string of codes, that an interruption in observing or recording is indicated with a semicolon, and that a session or string of sessions that is to be treated as a unit ends with a slash. Thus, for example, the deliberate breaks in recording for the !Kung infants, who were observed for six sessions, and the accidental breaks in recording that sometimes occurred in the joint attention study are both indicated with semicolons.

Sometimes several units may be defined for one subject, like repeated measures in an analysis of variance design. For example, children in the child distress study were observed during three different phases (preparation, insertion, and completion). The coding for each phase is treated as a different unit and hence slashes separate the data for each phase. Similarly, infants in the joint attention study were observed at three different ages, and so again slashes separate the data for each age. For better or worse, we often use the term *subject* because it is so familiar, but *unit*, or *sampling unit*, is often the more precise term.

A final note: The SDIS program limits the number of factors to 7, the number of levels per factor to 12, the number of subjects per design cell to 1,000, and the number of sessions per subject to 1,000. For most circumstances, we believe these limits are more than generous.

3.4 Names and comments

Both names and comments are optional. Names or other identifying information, enclosed in less-than and greater-than signs may be used to identify individual subjects (or subjects within conditions) if desired. Thus

<C12, Distressed.> *session*; *session* /

identifies data from the twelfth distressed couple, and

<#07, peer, 12-mo> *session*; *session*; *session* /

indicates data for the seventh infant, observed with a peer at 12 months of age, and

<#246, Prep> *session* / <#246, Insert> *session* /

identifies preparation and insertion data for a child from the child distress study. If it is ever necessary to examine the SDIS data file and make corrections, including identifying information along with the data usually proves helpful. Moreover, under some circumstances GSEQ prints these names along with summary statistics. Names are limited to 16 characters, including any blanks. They are placed before data associated with a subject's first session. If only a less-than sign appears on a line, SDIS assumes that the name extends to the end of the line, which is treated as an implicit closing greater-than sign. But note that if there are more than 16 characters before the end of the line, an error results.

Comments, enclosed in percent signs, can be placed anywhere in the file. For example,

<Subject 32> *session . . .*
session % possible malfunction % *session . . .*
session; *session* % equipment seems to be ok now
% guess the fix worked
more_sessions/

shows two comments embedded in subject 32's data. Such comments may be useful when examining the raw data file but are otherwise ignored. Note that comments, like names, need not be closed explicitly. If only one percent sign occurs on a line, the SDIS program assumes that the comment extends to the end of the line, which is treated as an implicit closing percent sign. If the comment continues on the following line, however, that line must begin with a percent. Comments are limited only by the length of the line.

3.5 Representing time

Information about time, including session start and stop times (for ESD, SSD, and TSD), state duration times (for SSD), and code onset and offset times (for TSD), is an important part of the SDIS data files. Only if you use ISD exclusively can you skip this section.

Times in SDIS files can be simple, like 32, or more complex, like 10:32 or even 10:32:48. More formally, times in SDIS files consist of one, two, or three numbers separated by either colons or periods. This generates seven possible forms, although most users will probably use only the first four or five. The seven permitted forms are:

1. *u* (e.g., 3, 82, or 4098)
2. *u:v* (e.g., 3:48)
3. *u:v:v* (e.g., 14:06:51)
4. *u.u* (e.g., 3.156)
5. *u:v.u* (e.g., 3:48.7)
6. *u.u.u*
7. *u.u:v*

where *v* represents any integer from 0 to 59 (numbers 60 or greater are regarded as an error) and *u* represents any integer from 0 to 65,535 (but entered without commas). For programming reasons, *u* needs to be limited to some maximum; 65,535 (2^{16}-1) is a convenient value and seems generous for most applications.

Any number after a colon is assumed to be one-sixtieth of the preceding number. Thus 3:48 could be 3 hours, 48 minutes or 3 minutes, 48 seconds, whereas 14:06:51 (or 14:6:51) could represent 14 hours, 6 minutes, 51 seconds. A simple number, the first number before a colon, or any number after a period is assumed to be decimal. Thus 3.156 means three and 156 thousandths, exactly as one would expect. In general, decimal numbers can represent any unit the user wishes (milliseconds, seconds, hours, days, etc.), although all times in a data file are assumed to represent the same units. The largest decimal number, as just noted, is limited to 65,535 (2^{16} - 1). In addition, the entire number (e.g., *u:v.u*), once reduced to the number of its rightmost units, is limited to 4,294,967,294 (2^{32} - 2).

Precision

The SDIS program infers precision from the first time value encountered in the data file and expects all time values thereafter to use exactly the same form. Thus, when using the *u.u* form, if any time in the file is expressed in thousandths (e.g., 5.234) then all times, including the first time given in the file, must indicate three digits after the decimal point (e.g., 2.000). Again, when using the *u:v* form, the first time given must be something like 8:00, not 8. If a simple number like 8 or 312 were encountered first (the *u* form), SDIS would assume precision at the whole integer level, and any other form used subsequently would be regarded as an error.

When using the *u.u* or *u:v.u* forms, it does not make sense to use more precision than is required or reasonable. For example, if the phenomena under study do not require greater than one-tenth of a second accuracy, do not enter times in the SDIS file in thousandths of a second, even if your recording device displays such values. Internally, SDIS and GSEQ treat state and timed event data as interval data. Thus if you specify thousandths of a second precision, SDIS and GSEQ create intervals each representing .001 of a second, and 1,000 are required per second. Thus, if you use thousandths of a second when tenths will do, SDIS and GSEQ will require more computer resources.

3.6 Session start and stop times

Explicit session start and stop times (i.e., session onset and offset times) are optional for event, state, and timed event data. You would include them for event sequences only if you wanted GSEQ to compute rates (see chapter 8). You would include them for state and timed event sequences if the session onset and offset times are different from those SDIS determines by default, as described in the next chapter. Start and stop times are not used and should not be given for interval sequences; if you were to include onset or offset times by mistake, the times would be regarded as codes instead. An error message would result if the times could not be interpreted as legal codes.

A comma precedes any explicit session start and stop times. Thus

,t

indicates a session start or stop time, whereas *t* represents time using any of the permissible forms just defined. For example,

,0

or

,0:00

at the beginning of a session indicates an onset or start time at zero units, whereas

,60

or

,1:00

indicates a start time at 60 units. Likewise,

,300

or

,5:00

at the end of a session indicates an offset or stop time of 300 units.

Normally, duration is computed exclusive of stop time. For example, the duration for a session that started at 2 and ended at 56 would be 54 units (see Fig. 3.1), and the duration for a session that started at 1:00 and ended at 5:00 would be 240 units. Some users may find it more natural to include the offset time in the duration, which is noted with a right parenthesis after the stop time. Thus

,t)

indicates an inclusive stop time. For example, if the start time is

,2

and the stop time is indicated as

,55)

then the duration would be 54 units (again, see Fig. 3.1).

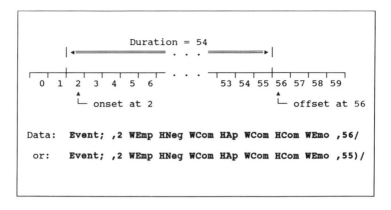

Figure 3.1. Event sequential data: An example of a session with an onset time
of 2 and an offset time of 56 (exclusive). W indicates wife, H indicates husband, and Com, Emo, Ap, Emp, and Neg indicate complain, emote, approve,
empathize, and negate, respectively (see chapter 2 for definitions). The first
interval marked represents second 0 (assuming a time unit of one second), the
second indicates second 1, and so forth; thus marks on the time line indicate
boundaries between successive time units.

3.7 Summary

Basic conventions for forming all four types of SDIS data files have been
presented in this chapter (see Tables 3.1 and 3.2). Information on how to
define behavioral codes, organize those codes into sessions, and, if
required, organize sessions into subjects and subjects into conditions has
been shown, in addition to how to identify the type of data and how to
include names and comments in the data file. This chapter also demonstrated how to represent time, using both decimal and sexagesimal conventions, and how to indicate session start and stop times if required.
This information is sufficient to form event sequential data files. Further

Table 3.1. *SDIS syntax for event sequences.*

Syntax	Interpretation
c	code
,t	session start time or exclusive stop time
,t)	inclusive session stop time

Table 3.2. *SDIS punctuation introduced in chapter 3.*

Mark	Interpretation
(. . .)	Parentheses may enclose sets of mutually exclusive and exhaustive codes. If present, they appear just after the initial data type declaration.
$	Set names begin with a dollar sign. Set names may be given to any sets of mutually exclusive and exhaustive codes listed just after the initial data type declaration.
=	An equals sign separates a set name from the codes in its set.
;	Semicolons separate the initial type declaration from the first session and any subsequent sessions from each other.
/	Slashes separate subjects (or sampling units). Thus the last (or only) session for a subject is terminated with a slash.
(. . .)	Parentheses enclose indices for the levels of a factorial design for a subject. If used in this way, they appear just before the terminating slash.
<. . .>	Less-than and greater-than signs enclose names that identify subjects, limited to 16 characters. If used, they are placed before data associated with a subject's first session.
%. . .%	Percent signs enclose comments. If used, they may appear anywhere in the data.
:	A semicolon signals that the number after it represent sixtieths, as for minutes or seconds. Used for time.
.	A period signals that the number after it is decimal. Used for time.
,	A comma signals that a time follows, for example, a session start or stop time, or separates indices of variable levels.
)	A right parenthesis after an offset time signals an inclusive (as opposed to an exclusive) offset time.

conventions are required to represent the timing of behaviors in state, timed event, and interval sequential data files. These conventions are presented in the next chapter.

4

Advanced SDIS: State, timed event, and interval data

Topics covered in this chapter include:

1. Syntax for the state duration times used in state sequential data.
2. Syntax for the momentary and duration behaviors used in timed event sequential data.
3. Default start and stop times for all four kinds of SDIS data.
4. Conventions and syntax for interval sequential data.

This chapter completes the work of presenting SDIS conventions begun in chapter 3. In particular, conventions required to represent the timing of behaviors in state, timed event, and interval sequential data files are described and demonstrated. A couple of the topics included in this chapter probably will be required by only a few users. They are labeled as advanced topics so that readers may skip them for now if they wish.

4.1 State times

If you do not plan to use SSD, you can skip this section. If you do use SSD, timing information for the states may be indicated by entering either onset times for the states or their durations in the SDIS file. Onset times for states, such as start and stop times for sessions, are preceded by commas. The onset time general form is

c,t

(or *code,onset_time*) and so

Un,0 Pe,2 Ob,5 Un,6 On,10 Ob,11 Un,13 ,18;

represents a session from the joint attention study that began at time 0, ended at time 18 (exclusive), lasted 18 time units (from 0 to 17), and consisted of a sequence of seven states (see Fig. 4.1). The inclusive form for session offset times, which in the present case would be 17 followed by a right parenthesis, may also be used. For states, the onset of the current state is the offset for the previous state. Thus the offset for the

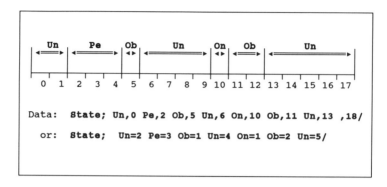

Figure 4.1. Single-stream state sequential data. An example of a session consisting of a single set of mutually exclusive and exhaustive codes. The session start time is 0 and the (inclusive) stop time is 17. Un, On, Pe, and Ob indicate unengaged, onlooking, person, and object, respectively (see chapter 2 for definitions). The first interval marked represents second 0 (assuming a time unit of one second), the second indicates second 1, and so forth.

first Un state in Figure 4.1 is time 2, which is the onset for the following Pe state.

Durations can be used instead of onset times, which some users find more convenient. An equals sign before a time indicates that a duration (instead of an onset or offset time) follows. The duration general form is

$c=t$

(or *code=duration_time*). Using this notation, the session depicted in Figure 4.1 would be represented as

Un=2 Pe=3 Ob=1 Un=4 On=1 Ob=2 Un=5;

An explicit session offset time is not needed; it is implied by the duration for the final Un state. Similarly, an explicit session onset time is not needed; it is always assumed to be zero. SDIS syntax for SSD is summarized in Table 4.1.

Table 4.1. *SDIS syntax for state sequences.*

Syntax	Interpretation
c,t	code, state onset time
c=t	code = state duration

Multiple streams of state sequences

The examples given in the previous paragraphs assumed a single set of mutually exclusive and exhaustive states, yet users may define several such sets. For example, one set might define an infant's actions and another the mother's. Or one set might define an animal's location and another the animal's activity. Each set is used to describe a separate, concurrent stream of activity.

Codes for each stream must be entered separately, using either the *c,t* or *c=t* form (forms cannot be mixed within a stream, although different streams may use different forms). Codes for different streams are separated with an ampersand (&). If using the *c=t* form for state sequences, the ampersand has the effect of resetting the session start time to zero so that the second set of codes can in effect be overlayed on the first. When using the *c,t* form for state sequences, the ampersand has the effect of momentarily turning off time checking. Normally, a state onset time that was the same as or less than the previous state's onset time would be regarded as an error. The ampersand allows the next onset time to violate this rule.

Other error checking remains in effect, however. Under most circumstances, the same code (or members of the same ME&E set) would not appear in different streams. Nonetheless, if they do, SDIS checks that the first onset time for the code in a stream is greater than the last offset time for that code (or for any code that is a member of the same ME&E set) in previous streams, and that ME&E codes do not overlap (provided the SDIS exclusivity check option is yes; see chapter 9).

An example of data coded using two ME&E sets of codes is given in Figure 4.2. The first set contains the codes A, B, C, and D and the second set contains the codes X, Y, and Z; thus the first line for the SSD file shown in Figure 4.2 would be

State (A B C D) (X Y Z);

It makes sense to declare these ME&E sets explicitly because then SDIS will perform appropriate error checking.

As mentioned in chapter 3, session stop times may be stated explicitly or determined by default (as described later in this chapter). If an explicit session stop time is given, and if more than one stream of states is coded, the stop time must follow the last stream, as in Figure 4.2. An explicit stop time entered before an ampersand is regarded as an error. The SDIS program imposes one further limitation – no more than 20 streams are permitted.

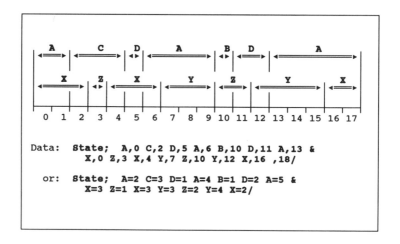

Figure 4.2. Multiple-stream state sequential data. An example of a session consisting of two sets of mutually exclusive and exhaustive codes. The session start time is 0 and the stop time is 17 (inclusive). The first interval marked represents second 0 (assuming a time unit of one second), the second indicates second 1, and so forth.

4.2 Times for momentary and duration behaviors

If you do not plan to use timed event sequential data, you can skip this section. For TSD, the duration of momentary behaviors (sometimes called frequency behaviors) is not of interest, by definition. Only their onset times are recorded. Insofar as duration is an issue, their duration is assumed to be one time unit. Thus momentary behaviors are represented exactly like states; the general form is

c,t

(or *code,onset_time*). For example,

Dtrs,22

indicates that code Dtrs occurred at time 22 and

Pras,3:42

indicates that code Pras occurred at 3 minutes and 42 seconds (or 3 hours and 42 minutes). Both are regarded as lasting one time unit.

Both onset and offset times are recorded for the duration behaviors that appear in timed event sequential data. Using a hyphen or minus sign, the general form is

$c,t_1\text{-}t_2$

(or *code,onset_time-offset_time*). Normally, duration is computed exclusive of offset time. For example,

Cry,1:45-1:51

indicates that code Cry lasted from 1:45 up to but not including 1:51, for a total duration of 6 units. The offset time must follow the hyphen directly; no intervening separators (blanks, etc.) are allowed (any separation following the hyphen signals to SDIS that the next number is a code, not a time). If a behavior lasts only one unit, only the onset time need be given (because duration defaults to one time unit), thus

Cope,16

and

Cope,16-17

are equivalent.

As you might expect, the inclusive form is allowed for behavior offset times, just as for session stop times. It is

$c,t_1\text{-}t_2)$

Thus

13,1:45-1:52

and

13,1:45-1:51)

are equivalent. For both, code 13 lasted 7 time units.

Sometimes the offset time for a code in a timed event sequential data file may be the onset time for the next behavior coded, as with states. If the user enters

$c,t\text{-}$

(with blanks or other separation characters after the hyphen) the SDIS program understands that the offset time for this code is the onset time for the next code, or the stop time for the session if no other codes follow. For example,

. . . Cry,238- GCon,247 . . .

is equivalent to

. . . Cry,238-247 GCon,247 . . .

and means that Cry lasted 9 time units. These and other conventions for momentary and duration behaviors as represented in timed event sequential data are demonstrated in Figure 4.3.

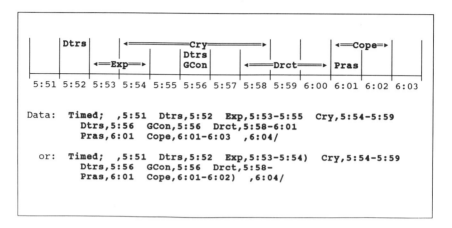

Figure 4.3. Timed event sequential data. An example of a session that began
at 5:51 and ended at 6:03 inclusive. The codes used are Cope, Dtrs (distress),
Cry, Exp (explain), Drct (distract), GCon (give control), and Pras (praise).
(See chapter 2 for definitions.) The first interval marked represents second
5:51 (assuming a time unit of one second), the second indicates second 5:52,
and so forth.

Two restrictions should be noted. First, although different codes may
co-occur (in both TSD and multiple stream SSD), identical codes may
not. Thus

... GCon,247 GCon,247 ...

and even

... Cry,238 Cry,238-251 ...

are regarded as errors by SDIS. Second, usually the c,t- form should not
be used before a *context code* (described in the next section): use the
c,t_1-t_2 form instead (unless you really intend the context code time to be
used as the undeclared offset time for the previous code).

It may occur to you that the c,t- form just described renders state
sequential data files unnecessary. SSD can be converted to TSD simply
by adding a hyphen to all state onset times. However, for users whose
data consist solely of states, adding hyphens to all onset times compli-
cates data entry; consequently we have preserved state sequential data as
a separate type. Moreover, the $c=t$ form is permitted only in state sequential data files.

Table 4.2. *SDIS syntax for timed event sequences.*

Syntax	Interpretation
c,t	momentary code, onset time
c,t_1-t_2	duration code, onset time–offset time
c,t_1-t_2)	duration code, onset time–inclusive offset time
c,t-	duration code, onset time (off implicitly by next onset)
$c,+t$	context code, onset time
$c,-t$	context code, offset time
$c,-t$)	context code, inclusive offset time

Timed context codes

Some behaviors may last a long time, in which case it may be easier to indicate onset and offset times at separate points in the data file. Such an approach is especially useful for contextual or situational information (e.g., in the laboratory, at night, when a stranger is present) that spans much or all of a session. Separated onset and offset times are signaled with plus and minus signs, respectively. Thus

$$c,+t_1$$

(or *context_code,+onset_time*) and

$$c,-t_2$$

(or *context_code,-offset_time*) indicates that code c began at time t_1 and ended at time t_2, respectively.

Usually a code that has been turned on with the $c,+t$ form will be turned off explicitly with a matching $c,-t$ form. As with other offset times, the inclusive form $c,-t$) may be used. If no matching offset time is found by the time the end-of-session semicolon (or the end-of-session slash for the subject's last session) is encountered, SDIS assumes that the offset times for those open codes is the session stop time. Hence contextual codes turned on at the beginning of a session are automatically turned off at the end. Similarly, if a $c,-t$ is encountered, and there is no earlier matching $c,+t$, then SDIS assumes that the onset time is the session start time. SDIS syntax for TSD is summarized in Table 4.2.

Context codes that are declared mutually exclusive and exhaustive at the outset (by being enclosed in parentheses; see chapter 3) automatically turn off other codes in the same set. Thus

> timed; . . .
> a,+3 . . . a,-24 b,+24 . . .

and

> timed (a b c); . . .
> a,+3 . . . b,+24 . . .

are equivalent. When context codes constitute ME&E sets, it makes sense to declare them as such because then, when one code is followed by another in the same set, you need enter only their onset times. However, codes may not be used both in the standard ways (i.e., using the c,t or c,t_1-t_2 or c,t- forms) and as context codes (i.e., using the $c,+t$ and $c,-t$ forms). Such mixed usage results in an error message. Had we allowed it, it would have been considerably more difficult to program the implicit offsets for sets of ME&E context codes as just described.

Multiple streams of timed event sequences

It is expected that codes will often overlap in timed event sequential data files. Still, the SDIS program expects codes to be entered sequentially and regards any onset time that is less than the onset time for the previous code as an error. Thus the codes in a TSD file are regarded as a single stream that flows forward, much like a single stream of state sequences but with overlapping events allowed. Under some circumstances, however, a user might wish to enter more than one stream of timed events. In such cases, an ampersand separates the two streams, as for state sequences. For example,

> . . . A,2:30-2:45 & B,1:28 . . .

would cause an error if the ampersand were not present. Sometimes it may be easier to enter a different person's behavior as a separate stream. Or it may be useful to separate context or *background codes* in a separate stream from *foreground codes*, as demonstrated in the next section.

Foreground and background timed events

As mentioned earlier, timed event sequential data can capture more of the complexity and richness of passing events than the other three data types defined here. For example, often investigators may want to code foreground events – momentary or duration behaviors of primary interest – and at the same time, may want to code background circumstances as well. Often such background circumstances or contextual factors have state-like properties and are naturally described with sets of mutually exclusive and exhaustive codes.

For example, imagine that turns of talk and other aspects of behavior are coded A, B, C, and so forth (and may co-occur), and that larger stretches of times are characterized by other, superordinate codes (X, Y, Z) representing aspects of the situation. Moreover, imagine that these contextual or situational codes are ME&E (e.g., father-present or father-absent). SDIS allows circumstances like these to be represented in at least two different ways. The context codes could be integrated into a single stream like this:

> timed A B C (X Y Z);
> X,+0:00 A,0:12-0:31 B,0:18 . . . Y,+5:32 A,5:56-6:12 . . .

or presented in a separate stream like this:

> timed A B C (X Y Z);
> A,0:12-0:31 B,0:18 . . . A,5:56-6:12 . . . &
> X,+0:00 Y,+5:32 . . .

whichever seems more convenient.

4.3 Defaults for session start and stop times

This section applies to ESD, SSD, and TSD. For event sequential data, session start and stop times are optional; you would include them in an event sequential data file only if you intend to ask GSEQ to compute rates later on (see Fig. 3.1, also chapter 8), thus no defaults are provided.

For state sequential data using the $c=t$ form, the session start time defaults to zero and the stop time is determined from the accumulated state durations; in this case, there is no need to enter start and stop times (see Fig. 4.1). For state sequential data using the c,t form and for timed event sequential data, session start and stop times are important and typically would be entered explicitly in the SDIS data file (see Fig. 4.3). If you do not enter a start time, zero is assumed (as in Fig. 4.1), and if you fail to enter a stop time, it defaults to one greater than the onset time for the last state (SSD) or to the exclusive offset time for the last event (TSD). Thus if the data shown in Figure 4.1 had ended with

> Un,13;

instead of

> Un,13 ,18;

the exclusive session stop time would have defaulted to 14.

As noted earlier, start and stop times are not used with interval sequential data, and so the issue of defaults does not arise.

Dual session start times (advanced topic)

Normally all times in a session are regarded as relative to the session start time. Thus if the session start time is 10:00, the time 10:12 occurs at time unit 13, 12 units after the start time. Under some circumstances it may be desirable to assume a start time of zero for code onset and offset times and allow session start and stop times to reflect other times, perhaps the actual time of day (e.g., you might want to preserve the time of day when observations occurred while collecting data with a stopwatch that is reset to zero for each session). This is accomplished with an asterisk after the session start time, and so the general form is

,t*

If the session start time is followed by an asterisk, then the session stop time is assumed to be relative to the session start time, but all other times are assumed to be relative to zero. For example,

,10:20 Cry,10:22-10:36 Dstrc,10:33 Cope,11:34- ,12:00;

is equivalent to

,10:20* Cry,0:2-0:16 Dstrc,0:13 Cope,1:14-1:40 ,12:00;

Usually the asterisk convention, if used at all, would be used for timed event sequential data, but it could also be used for state sequential data expressed using the *c,t* form.

4.4 Interval sequential data

If you do not plan to use ISD, you can skip this section. As noted earlier, interval sequences are quite different from event, state, and timed event sequences. Rather than recording events and the times they occur, the presence of events is recorded at specified times, usually at the end of specified intervals. Thus the recording interval is a critical part of the definition of any interval sequential data file. It is specified with an equals sign, so its general form is

=w

where w represents interval duration, expressed as a simple number (no decimals or colons are permitted, except for subintervals, as described later). This specification is given immediately after the word Interval at the start of an ISD file. For example,

Interval =15 . . .

indicates an interval duration of 15 time units. It remains in effect for all sessions in the file. The default interval duration is 1; if no =w appears after Interval, an interval duration of 1 is assumed.

A comma indicates interval boundaries. For example,

IOfr ISmi, XOfr, XEnt IVoc, , IVoc;

places codes IOfr and ISmi in interval one, XOfr in interval two, XEnt and IVoc in interval three, no codes in interval four, and IVoc in interval five. This brief session ends with a semicolon: common to all data types, including ISD, is the end-of-session semicolon, the end-of-subject slash, and the condition indices enclosed in parentheses, as described in chapter 3.

Replicating intervals

The same code or codes, or lack of codes, may characterize several successive intervals. In this case, rather than repeat the same information, a replication number can be indicated with an asterisk. Specifically,

*n

indicates that all codes in the present interval characterize not just the present interval but n intervals. For example,

IVoc XEnt *2, XOfr, ISmi, *4, IVoc;

is equivalent to

IVoc XEnt, IVoc XEnt, XOfr, ISmi, , , , , IVoc;

No other codes can follow the *n specification. If present, it must be the last piece of information for the interval.

Interval context codes

Some relatively long-lasting codes, like contextual or situational codes, may characterize all or most of the intervals in a session. In such cases, you may prefer to indicate onset and offset separately, in a manner analogous to the $c,+t$ and $c,-t$ forms defined for time sequential data. For interval sequential data, a plus sign following a code turns the code on, so its general form is

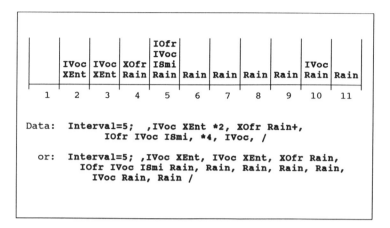

Figure 4.4. Interval sequential data. An example of a session showing normal interval codes, replicated intervals, and a contextual code (Rain, closed automatically by end of session). The other codes used are IOfr, ISmi, IVoc, XOfr, and XEnt for infant offers, smiles, and vocalizes, and other offers and entertains, respectively (see chapter 2 for definitions). The first interval marked represents interval 1, the second interval 2, and so forth.

$c+$

The code is regarded as on for the present interval and in all successive intervals until it is turned off explicitly, another context code that is a member of the same ME&E set is turned on, or the end of session occurs.

Similarly, a hyphen or minus sign following a code turns the code off explicitly, so its general form is

$c-$

The code is regarded as off for the present interval but on for all previous intervals back to and including the interval that contained the initial matching $c+$. (For technical reasons, the start of the session may serve as an implicit onset for TSD but not ISD context codes; a lone $c-$ in an ISD file is regarded as an error.) As you might expect, an inclusive form,

$c-)$

is also defined. The code is regarded as still on for the present interval, as for previous intervals, but then off in successive intervals. These and other ISD conventions are demonstrated in Figure 4.4 and SDIS syntax for ISD is summarized in Table 4.3.

Table 4.3. *SDIS syntax for interval sequences.*

Syntax	Interpretation
=w	=interval duration
*n	*replication number
c+	context code onset (on in this and following intervals)
c-	context code offset (off in this interval)
c-)	context code inclusive offset (off in next interval)

Sampling (advanced topic)

Different sampling strategies can be used to collect interval sequences, and these strategies can have implications for a variety of computations (see Altmann, 1974; Suen & Ary, 1989; Quera, 1990). Three types of sampling strategies commonly defined are:

1. *Momentary* (also called instantaneous). As with a snapshot, the observer records the state of affairs as of a single, essentially instantaneous point in time.
2. *Partial interval* (also called zero-one). The observer notes whether specified behaviors occurred at some point during the interval. Behaviors that occurred only once or several times are both coded as present.
3. *Whole interval.* The observer notes whether specified behaviors occurred during the entire interval. Behaviors that did not occur or did not occupy the entire interval are both coded as absent.

Sampling strategy needs to be specified only if the user plans to use analysis programs that take it into account (in GSEQ, only the DURA specification on the Simple command when used with ISD is affected; see chapter 8). The default is momentary. Thus

Interval =10 . . .

indicates an interval duration of 10 time units with momentary sampling. Partial and whole interval sampling are indicated with a single quote and a double quote after the interval duration, respectively. Thus

Interval = 10′ . . .

indicates an interval duration of 10 time units with partial interval sampling whereas

Interval = 10" . . .

indicates an interval duration of 10 time units with whole interval sampling.

For the !Kung infants study described in chapter 2, Konner recorded the stream of events as he saw them, inserting a mark every five seconds. Thus his procedure does not completely fit any of the three kinds of sampling defined here. Partly for simplicity, and partly because Konner's time interval of five seconds is quite fine relative to the behaviors he recorded, we decided to regard his sampling as essentially momentary for the examples and analyses presented here. When in doubt, it is usually best to assume momentary sampling.

Observing and recording subintervals (advanced topic)

Sometimes observers using partial or whole interval sampling, especially those who rely on pencil and paper recording procedures, may divide the interval into an observing period and a recording period. If this is the case, and if analysis programs that take this distinction into account are to be used (which GSEQ currently does not), then the subintervals need to be specified. Like an undivided interval duration, durations for the observing and recording intervals follow an equals sign, except that the subintervals are separated by a period, so its general form is

$=x.y$

where x indicates the observing subinterval and y the recording subinterval. The duration for the entire interval is the sum of the durations for the two subintervals.

4.5 Summary

This chapter completes the presentation of SDIS conventions (see Table 4.4). We now have demonstrated how to form all four types of SDIS data files. In particular, we have shown how to represent behavioral codes and their onset and offset (or duration) times, as appropriate. SDIS data files, of course, are only a means to an end. In the next chapter we begin to explain how the GSEQ program operates on SDIS data files to produce simple frequencies, conditional probabilities, and other basic sequential statistics.

Table 4.4. *SDIS punctuation introduced in chapter 4.*

Mark	Interpretation
=	An equals sign signals that a state duration time follows (for SSD), or that an interval duration follows (for ISD).
&	An ampersand separates different streams of states or timed events (for SSD and TSD). In effect, it turns sequential time checking off for the time associated with the next code entered (provided that the code does not overlap with itself or any member of its ME&E set entered in a previous stream).
-	A hyphen or minus sign between two times separates an onset from an offset time (for TSD). The offset time must follow directly with no intervening separating characters.
+	A plus sign after a code and a comma and before a time signals an onset time that will be turned off later (for TSD), or the onset of a code that will be turned off in a later interval (for ISD).
-	A hyphen or minus sign after a code and a comma and before a time signals an offset time for a code turned on earlier (for TSD), or the offset of a code that was turned on in some earlier interval (for ISD).
*	An asterisk before a number indicates a replication factor (for ISD).
,	A comma signals interval boundaries (for ISD).

Advanced Topics

*	An asterisk after a session start time signals that times in the session are relative to zero (advanced topic, for TSD and perhaps SSD).
'	A single quote after an interval duration signals partial interval sampling (advanced topic, ISD only).
"	A double quote after an interval duration signals whole interval sampling (advanced topic, ISD only).
.	A period between two interval durations separates an observing from a recording interval (advanced topic, ISD only).

5

Basic GSEQ: Specifying target and given codes

Topics covered in this chapter include:

1. The general format for GSEQ commands.
2. The File command, which is used to specify which SDIS data files are to be processed by GSEQ.
3. The Rename command, which is used to rename codes in an SDIS file for the duration of a GSEQ run.
4. The Title command, which is used to label analyses in the GSEQ output file.
5. The Target and Given commands, which are used to specify the two-dimensional contingency tables GSEQ extracts from SDIS data files.
6. The Lag command, which specifies whether target behaviors are lagged relative to given behaviors.

This chapter presents basic GSEQ commands. Commands are organized in a file, which might look something like this:

```
FILE "mydata";
TITLE "Example GSEQ command file";
STATS JNTF EXPF XSQ;
TARGET HCom HEmo HApp HEmp HNeg HOth;
LAG 1;
GIVEN WCom WEmo WApp WEmp WNeg WOth;
END;
```

although only the File and Target commands are absolutely required, and the Given command is required only when given behaviors are different from target ones, as explained shortly.

Some commands are used to specify the data file, others to identify separate analyses of that data set, but the Target and Given commands introduced here are central to the computational work of GSEQ because they define the columns and rows of the two-dimensional contingency tables that GSEQ extracts from the SDIS data files. No matter what the

46

unit of analysis or tallying unit is – whether events (ESD), or time units (SSD and TSD), or intervals (ISD) – the rows and columns of those tables are labeled with the codes specified on Target and Given commands.

Often the codes used are those already residing in the SDIS data file. Thus, for example, you might ask how many times negates follows complains at lag 1 (ESD), or how many seconds (assuming 1-second time units) are coded for both child copes and adult distracts (TSD). But there are other possibilities as well. In chapter 6, we describe a number of data modification commands, which create new codes from existing ones. And in chapter 7 we describe an additional and particularly powerful data modification command (the Window command), which allows you to define a new code that encompasses a period of time (or a stretch of intervals) keyed to onsets and/or offsets of existing codes. Used primarily with TSD, it allows you to ask, for example, how often an offset of child cries occurred within 10 seconds of an onset of adult distracts.

5.1 Creating GSEQ command files

GSEQ command files are standard ASCII files that contain commands understood by the GSEQ program. Like SDIS data files, command files can be created using any word processor or editor that can save to an ASCII (or text) file. These files consist of as many lines as are required to specify the work you want GSEQ to do.

In general, commands consist of a word identifying the command followed by parameters and terminated by a semicolon, so their general form is

COMMAND parameters ;

As with SDIS data files, there are no fixed columns. Commands may be entered anywhere on a line, and may span more than one line if necessary. The command is not case sensitive; thus, for example, FILE, File, and file are all equivalent. Parameters are separated with spaces (or the end of line, if the command spans more than one line). As many spaces as desired may be used to separate commands and parameters. In theory, there is no limit to the length of a line but in practice lines limited to a width that is easily displayed or printed are strongly recommended.

The terminating semicolon may be made optional if you wish (by setting the GSEQ semicolons option to *no*; see chapter 9). However, then codes in the SDIS file cannot be given the same names as GSEQ *reserved words* (i.e., GSEQ command names or any of their named parameters; see Appendix B). If you accept the default (semicolons option set *yes*), code names are not restricted but every GSEQ command must end with a semicolon.

Comments

Comments, enclosed in percent signs, may be embedded anywhere in the command file (exactly like comments in SDIS data files). For example,

> FILE . . .
> % specifications for AGS's thesis
> *GSEQ_specifications*
> % modified September 4 % *more_GSEQ_specifications*

shows two embedded comments. The first is closed implicitly by the end of the line and the second is closed explicitly. Such comments can provide useful documentation but otherwise are ignored.

The End command

GSEQ assumes that the command file ends with the last line. For clarity, the last command may be

> END { ; }

which unambiguously marks the end of the GSEQ command file. As a general convention, used throughout this book, optional elements are enclosed in braces, so here the End command may be followed by a semicolon or not, as you wish.

The File command

The File command identifies a data file and must be the first line in the GSEQ command file. Its general form is

> FILE "*filename*" { *options* } ;

where *filename* follows standard DOS rules and must be enclosed in double quotes. If no path is provided before *filename*, GSEQ searches the current directory. If no extension is provided, GSEQ assumes MDS (the extension given the modified SDIS file created when an error-free SDIS file is processed).

   Almost always, the form used for the File command is

> FILE "*filename*" ;

omitting both the three-character extension of the complete filename and any options. In that case, GSEQ assumes that earlier the SDIS program processed the file named *filename*.SDS (where *filename* is any name you select, as long as it follows DOS rules for naming files), found no errors, and consequently created a file named *filename*.MDS. The contents of the SDS (or SDIS) version of the file were described in chapters 3 and 4 and are designed to be easily readable by humans, whereas the MDS version is designed to be efficient for GSEQ processing. Procedures for using the SDIS program to convert SDS to MDS files are described in chapter 9. For a description of how the File command works when *filename*.MDS does not exist, and the options that might be specified in that case, see Appendix B.

Users may analyze data from more than one data file during a GSEQ run. In such cases, several File commands might appear in the GSEQ command file, each followed by commands that refer to and analyze the data in that file.

The Rename command

If you are happy with the names of your codes as they appear in the SDIS file, you will probably not use this command. Normally GSEQ refers to codes as they appear in the SDIS file and uses those names as labels for output. Thus code Un is named and labeled Un, code WCom is named and labeled WCom, and so forth. Sometimes users may prefer that GSEQ use different names, however, and these can be provided with the Rename command. Its general form is

RENAME *new_code1* = *old_code1* . . . ;

For example,

RENAME Unoccupied = Un;

would provide a more informative name for code Un. The Rename command is especially useful when, in order to save space in the SDIS data file, simple numeric codes are used. Thus

RENAME Unoccupied=1 Onlooker=2 Person=3 Object=4
Joint=5;

lets GSEQ use more understandable names and labels for codes that, in the SDIS file, are simply the digits 1 through 5. Not all codes need be renamed, of course; those that are not retain their original name.

If a Rename command is used, it is placed immediately after a File command. Only one Rename command may be specified per File command. If any of the old codes on the Rename command do not occur in the file named on the File command, an error message is printed. We recommend limiting names for new codes to 7 characters (although up to

16 are allowed) because GSEQ only displays the first 7. The new codes remain in effect, and are used instead of the old codes for all subsequent commands (like the Target and Given commands described in later sections), until the next File command or until the end of the run. Thus the effect of the Rename command is temporary; it does not affect the SDIS data file (unless a modified file is saved; see chapter 6). However, once a new code has been named on the Rename command, a reference to an old code is an error.

5.2 Specifying contingency tables of given and target behaviors

Almost all of the analyses GSEQ performs are based on two-dimensional contingency tables. Thus defining the rows (representing *given* behaviors) and columns (representing *target* behaviors) for these tables, whose cells GSEQ subsequently fills with the appropriate counts, is of fundamental importance.

Rows are labeled with the codes listed on the Given command and columns with the codes listed on the Target command, which looks like this:

```
        GIVEN              TARGET BEHAVIORS
      BEHAVIORS       code A    code B    code C
                  ┌─────────┬─────────┬─────────┐
       code X     │         │         │         │
                  ├─────────┼─────────┼─────────┼──
       code Y     │         │         │         │
                  ├─────────┼─────────┼─────────┤
                  │         │         │
                  │         │         │
```

The meaning of the frequencies in individual cells, however, depends on the tallying unit or the unit of analysis. The units classified and tallied are *events* for event sequences, *time units* for state and timed event sequences, and *intervals* for interval sequences.

The time relation or lag between givens (rows) and targets (columns) is assumed to be zero unless otherwise specified (using the Lag command). By convention, we think of target behaviors as being consequent to (i.e., occurring after) given behaviors. Usually lags are specified only for ESD and ISD, whereas time windows (see chapter 7) accomplish a similar purpose for SSD and TSD.

Target and given behaviors are defined with the Target and Given commands, respectively. For each pair of Target and Given commands supplied by the user, GSEQ produces by default one table for each subject represented in the SDIS data file. Additional tables may be printed for each subject if more than one lag is requested, as described shortly. It is also possible to produce tables separately for each session (the default is to pool over sessions within subjects) or to pool over subjects within each cell of the design (if there is one), or to pool over selected factors of the design, or even to pool over all subjects and all levels of all factors, thus producing a single table (assuming no lags). Specifications to accomplish such pooling are described in chapter 8.

In this chapter we focus on target and given specifications, leaving such topics as data modification (including defining time windows keyed to onsets and offsets of existing codes), pooling, and statistical computations to the next three chapters. In particular, users who wish to identify periods of time keyed to the onsets and/or offsets of particular codes in TSD (Did an adult distract an infant within five seconds of the onset of infant crying?), or who wish to identify targets or givens that span more than one interval in ISD (Did the infant vocalize either in the same interval that an adult did or in the following one?), should use the Window command to define a new code, as described in chapter 7.

The Title command

If you wish, tables and other information written to GSEQ's output file may be given a title. Thus

TITLE "*title*" ;

prints *title* on each page of output, where *title* is any string of characters, including blanks. The title must be enclosed in double quotes and applies to all subsequent tables, as specified by the Target and Given commands described in the next section, until a new title is supplied. Titles are limited to 80 characters.

5.3 Using Target, Given, and Lag commands

All GSEQ command files include at least one Target command and, unless the given behaviors are the same as the target ones, a Given command as well. The lag command is used only if you wish to investigate lagged associations (as opposed to concurrent ones), usually with event sequential data.

The general form for the Target command is

TARGET *codes* ;

and for the Given command is

GIVEN *codes* ;

As many as 20 codes may be listed. Additional notation is allowed on Target and Given commands as well, and is described later in this chapter.

Lags are specified with the Lag (or Lags) command. If present, it immediately follows the Target command. Its general form is

LAG *lag* { *lag* . . . } { TO *lag* } ;

where *lag* is an integer between -100 and +100 inclusive, and braces enclose optional information. Multiple lags are separated with blanks, not commas. The number of different lags that may be entered, either explicitly or implicitly by means of TO, is limited to 20.

If no Lag command is found, GSEQ assumes a lag of zero. Otherwise, the target codes are lagged relative to the given codes. In general, we find it is less confusing and more natural to think of antecedent behaviors as givens and consequent behaviors as targets. For that reason, we decided that lags should refer to codes named on the Target and not the Given command. Thus given behaviors always occur at lag 0, by definition. Because given behaviors occur at lag 0 and target behaviors are usually thought of as consequent, lags for target behaviors are usually positive integers like +1.

For example, using event codes from the marital talk study,

TARGET HCom HEmo HAp HEmp HNeg HOth;
LAG +1;
GIVEN WCom WEmo WAp WEmp WNeg WOth;

defines the six husband codes as targets. The lag is +1 (the plus sign is optional for positive integers), which for event sequential data means that the investigator is interested in events (targets) that follow other events (givens) immediately. The six wife codes from the marital talk study are defined as givens. Together, these three commands specify the following two-dimensional, 6 × 6 table.

GIVENS Lag 0	TARGETS, Lag 1					
	HCom	HEmo	HAp	HEmp	HNeg	HOth
WCom						
WEmo						
WAp						
WEmp						
WNeg						
WOth						

Rows are defined by the six wife behaviors at lag 0 and columns by the six husband behaviors at lag +1. The individual cells would then contain tallies, for example, for the number of times wife complaining was followed by husband complaining (cell in upper left-hand corner), along with any other statistics the user requested (see chapter 8).

One Target command is required for each table desired. The Lag and Given commands are optional, but if present, must occur in the order Target, Lag, Given. If the Given command is absent, then GSEQ assumes that the given codes are the same as the target ones. For example, using state codes from the joint attention study,

> TARGET Un On Pe Ob Jt; LAG 2;
> GIVEN Un On Pe Ob Jt;

and

> TARGET Un On Pe Ob Jt; LAG 2;

are equivalent.

More than one lag may be specified. For example, using interval codes from the !Kung infants study,

> TARGET IVoc; LAG 0 1 2;
> GIVEN XVoc;

signals that the investigator wants to know how often, given that the other person vocalized in an interval, the infant vocalized in the same interval (lag 0), in the following interval (lag 1), and after one intervening interval (lag 2). The keyword TO can also be used. Thus,

> LAG 0 TO 3;

indicates lags 0, 1, 2, and 3. (Note: only one number can follow TO but more than one might precede it.) As noted earlier, if no Lag command follows the Target command, a lag of zero is assumed.

Although lags are usually positive, they need not be; thus relations between given behaviors that occur after target behaviors could be examined by specifying negative lags. For example,

> TARGET HCom HNeg; LAG -1; GIVEN WAp;

requests that GSEQ determine how often husband complains and negates preceded wife approving. Similar, usually identical information is produced by

> TARGET WAp; LAG +1; GIVEN HCom HNeg;

which requests that GSEQ determine how often wife approves follows husband complains and negates. But no matter whether investigators think in terms of positive or negative lags, GSEQ provides appropriate syntax.

Lags and data types

Under most circumstances, lags would always be specified for event sequences (ESD), sometimes for interval sequences (ISD), and almost never for state or timed event sequences (SSD or TSD). Even so, GSEQ tends to be a permissive program. It allows investigators to include any command that makes syntactic sense, even if it does not make sense when used with a particular data file. For example, a lag of zero could be specified for event sequences, but because such data consist of a single stream of codes that by definition cannot co-occur, all lag 0 tallies would be zero. Again, lags other than zero could be specified for state or timed event sequences, but the lags would refer to the time unit used, which often is too fine a unit to be useful as a lag. As noted earlier, in such cases investigators would probably use the data modification command for stretches (or windows) of time keyed to onsets and offsets of existing codes, as defined in chapter 7.

Specifying all codes or sets of codes

Instead of specific codes, a set name or an asterisk can be used on Target and Given commands, where the asterisk represents all codes used in the SDIS data file. As many as 20 different codes may be implied. Taking this syntax into account, the general forms for Target and Given commands are

TARGET [*codes* | * | $*set_name*] ;

and

GIVEN [*codes* | * | $*set_name*] ;

where a straight line separates choices and choices in brackets are mandatory. For example, assuming that the data file for the joint attention study began with

State ($JAS = Un On Pe Ob Jt); . . .

and that the file contains only these five codes, then

TARGET $JAS;

and

TARGET *;

and

TARGET Un On Pe Ob Jt;

would all be equivalent. The asterisk would normally be used only when the codes in a data file constitute a single set of mutually exclusive and exhaustive (ME&E) codes, which is true for codes in event sequential files by definition, in state sequential files consisting of a single stream, and in interval sequential files if only one code per interval is permitted. As a general rule, users should always ask themselves whether an asterisk on a Target command makes sense, given the codes in the data.

Using the residual code

An ampersand (&) may follow other codes (or the asterisk, or set name) on the Target and Given commands. If present, it represents *and everything else not named*. Any unit tallied (event, time unit, or interval) that does not match one of the codes explicitly or implicitly listed matches the residual code by definition. Taking this syntax into account, the general forms for the Target and Given commands are

TARGET [*codes* | * | *$set_name*] { & } ;

and

GIVEN [*codes* | * | *$set_name*] { & } ;

where the ampersand is optional. As usual, no more than 20 codes, not counting the ampersand, may be listed or implied. For example, for the event sequences from the marital talk study,

TARGET HCom &;

categorizes target events as either husband complaining or husband not complaining, whereas for the state sequences from the joint attention study

TARGET Ob Jt &;

categorizes target time units as either object play, joint play, or something other than object or joint play. Finally, for the interval sequences from the !Kung infants study

TARGET ISmi &;

categorizes target intervals as coded for infant smiling or not, and for the timed event sequences from the child distress study

TARGET Cry &;

categorizes target time units as coded for cry or not.

Only codes of immediate interest need be specified on Target and Given commands. Thus, assuming event sequential data,

TARGET HCom HNeg; LAG 1; GIVEN WCom;

specifies that only lag 1 transitions from wife complains to husband complains or negates will be tallied, and, assuming state sequential data,

TARGET Ob Jt; LAG 1; GIVEN On Pe;

specifies that only time units coded onlooking or person engagement followed by time units coded object or joint play will be tallied. Thus the first pair of Target and Given commands would exclude all precursors of husband complains and negates other than wife complains, whereas the second would exclude all transitions into object or joint play that were not from onlooking or person engagement.

Such limited lists are usually unwise. For each pair of Target and Given commands, GSEQ constructs a two-dimensional table. There are as many columns as there are codes on the Target command; likewise, the number of rows is determined by the number of codes on the Given command (in this case, the ampersand counts as a code). Normally, GSEQ would determine not just tallies for individual cells but a number of other statistics as well (see chapter 8). Many of these depend on the number of tallies in the table as a whole, and so tables that exclude much of the data due to limited lists on Target and Given commands may produce statistics that at best are difficult to interpret, and at worst are simply meaningless. As a general rule, then, lists should be *exhaustive*, either because they comprise a mutually exclusive and exhaustive set of codes (e.g., all husband event codes, or all infant state codes), or because the ampersand is used to reserve a row or column for the set of all events, time units, or intervals not otherwise listed.

5.4 Hierarchical processing of target and given codes

No matter whether lists of codes on Target and Given commands are exhaustive with respect to a particular dimension, GSEQ treats them as mutually exclusive. In other words, each unit tallied is assigned to one, and only one, column and row; doing anything else violates basic rules of contingency table formation and renders contingency table statistics such as chi-square meaningless.

If the data consist of a single stream of codes (either events, states, or intervals), no problems arise. GSEQ examines each unit in the sequence. If no code on the target list matches the code for that unit, the unit is ignored; likewise for the given list. Otherwise a tally is added to the cell defined by the row and column for the matching given and target code, respectively. No conflicts can occur. Each unit consists of or contains a single code and so only one code on the target list and one on the given list can match.

However, if the data consist of co-occurring codes (either multiple streams of states, or timed event sequences, or interval sequences), conflicts can occur and are resolved in favor of codes occurring earlier on the list. If a unit contains more than one code, first a match is sought with the first code on the target list, then the second code on the list, and so forth; likewise for the given list. Some rule is needed to ensure that no unit will cause a tally to be added to more than one cell, and a hierarchical rule, giving precedence to items listed first, seems as reasonable as any.

For example, if the user specified

>   TARGET ISmi IVoc &;

and if infant smiling and vocalizing both occurred in the same interval, a tally would be added only to the ISmi and not the IVoc column. Similarly, if a state sequential file consisted of two sets of ME&E codes, and the SDIS file began with

>   State (A C E F) (M N P);

and if the user specified

>   TARGET A M P &;

then GSEQ would assign every time unit coded A to column A (whether or not it was also coded M or P), every time unit coded M (but not A) to column M, every time unit coded P (but neither A nor M) to column P, and every time unit coded neither A nor M nor P to the residual or ampersand column.

Coding conflicts can never arise if a single code is coupled with an ampersand; such "A, not-A" combinations are necessarily mutually exclusive. Thus, using codes for timed events from the child distress study,

>   TARGET Cope &;
>   GIVEN Exp &;

requests that GSEQ determine how many time units were coded for both child cope and adult explain, for just child cope, for just adult explain, and for neither; whereas, using interval codes from the !Kung infants study,

>   TARGET IVoc &;
>   GIVEN XVoc &;

requests that GSEQ determine how many intervals were coded for both infant and other, just infant, just other, and neither vocalizing.

Table 5.1. *GSEQ punctuation introduced in chapter 5.*

Mark	Interpretation
;	Semicolons may be used to terminate commands.
% . . . %	Percent signs enclose optional comments. They may appear anywhere in the file.
=	Equals signs separate new codes from old codes for the Rename command.
+	A plus sign indicates a positive lag. It may be omitted.
-	A hyphen or minus sign indicates a negative lag.
*	An asterisk may be used on the Target and Given commands. It indicates that targets or givens include all codes appearing in the data file.
&	An ampersand may follow codes on the Target and Given commands. It signifies a residual code or category.
$	A dollar sign must precede any set names used on the Target and Given commands.

Table 5.2. *GSEQ commands introduced in chapter 5.*

Command	Parameters
FILE	"*filename*" { *options* } ;
RENAME	*new_code1* = *old_code1* . . . ;
TITLE	"*title*" ;
TARGET	[*codes*	*	$*set_name*] { & } ;
LAG	*lag* { *lag* . . . } { TO *lag* } ;
GIVEN	[*codes*	*	$*set_name*] { & } ;
END	{ ; }

Note: A vertical line separates choices. Choices enclosed in braces are optional; choices enclosed in brackets are mandatory.

5.5 Summary

Basic conventions for the GSEQ program have been presented in this chapter (see Tables 5.1 and 5.2). We showed how to identify the data file to be analyzed and how to rename the codes in the data file using the Rename command. We also demonstrated how to title output and identify simple given and target behaviors with particular codes, lagged and unlagged as desired. The simplicity and flexibility of GSEQ commands and the usefulness of the residual code have been demonstrated. The next two chapters show how to modify the data initially contained in the SDIS file, producing new, often quite useful codes in addition to those already defined.

6
Modifying SDIS data

Topics covered in this chapter include:

1. How to use the Recode command to give any of several existing codes a single name, thereby creating a new, superordinate category.
2. How to use the Lump and Chain commands to create new codes from existing sequences (used primarily for codes within mutually exclusive and exhaustive sets).
3. How to use the Lump command to remove repeated codes from event, state, and timed event sequences, if desired.
4. How to remove codes from consideration altogether using the Remove command.
5. How to use the And, Or, Not, Nor, and Xor commands to create new codes from existing, co-occurring codes.
6. How to remove information concerning onset and offset times from state and timed event sequences, thereby creating an event sequential version of more complex data streams.
7. How to save a modified data file for future use.

SDIS distinguishes, and GSEQ analyzes, four kinds of data. We find this categorization into event, state, timed event, and interval sequences extremely useful, as we think this book demonstrates, but we also recognize that boundaries can occasionally become hazy. For example, event sequences, a single stream of states, and multiple streams of states are alike in that their codes all represent one or more sets of mutually exclusive and exhaustive codes. Further, multiple streams of states, timed events, and interval sequences that permit more than one code per interval are alike in that all allow co-occurrences to be expressed. In addition to distinctions among the four basic data types, the two distinctions just mentioned (codes expressed as ME&E sets or not, co-occurrences permitted or not) affect the commands used for data modification. Some of the data modification commands presented in this chapter are used primarily when codes fall into ME&E sets, whereas others are used only to recode co-occurring behaviors.

A number of data modification commands are presented in this chapter. If encountered in the GSEQ command file, they affect the internal representation of the data created when the last File command was encountered. They do not affect the permanent version of the data (which presumably remains safely on disk) unless the modified version is saved (the Save command is described later in this chapter). Several different data modification commands may follow each other. Their effect is cumulative; the first modifies the internal representation, the second modifies the modified internal representation, and so forth.

Thus data modification commands, if present, affect the data analyzed by subsequent Target and Given commands. It is even possible that other data modification commands might follow those Target and Given commands, which in turn would be followed by still more Target and Given commands. But remember, the second set of data modification commands would operate on data as modified by the first set. If for some reason you want to return to the unmodified data before making a second set of modifications, then reissue the File command. This has the effect of refreshing the internal representation of the data from the permanent (disk) version.

Data modification commands create new codes from old. As you would expect, the old codes must be known to the SDIS file, either occurring in it or being declared explicitly.

6.1 Creating superordinate codes

Occasionally it is useful to recode some of the codes present in the original SDIS data file for a single analysis or series of analyses. An investigator might want to form a single new category from several existing codes, for example, or regard a particular sequential pattern as a named code, whose relations to other codes can then be investigated. Such dynamic recoding is one of the more useful features of GSEQ. It is in effect only for a particular GSEQ run and, unless saved, does not alter the original SDIS or MDS data file. As you would expect, any of the new codes created by recoding can be used on Target and Given commands wherever an initial code might appear.

The Recode command

A new code or category can be formed from existing codes using the Recode command. Its general form is

RECODE *new_code* = *codes* ;

It is a simple and straightforward command that can be used with all four of the basic SDIS data types. Whenever any of the codes to the right of the equals sign occurs, it is treated as an occurrence of the new code defined to the left of the equals sign. As many as 20 existing codes may be listed, in any order. The name for the new code follows the usual rules for naming codes given in chapter 3.

For example, the command

RECODE Alone = Un Ob;

would change the state sequence

Un=2 Pe=3 Ob=1 Un=4 On=1 Ob=2 Un=5 . . .

into the new state sequence

Alone=2 Pe=3 Alone=1 Alone=4 On=1 Alone=2 Alone=5 . . .

Similarly, the command

RECODE AAct = Exp Drct GCon Pras;

would change the timed event sequence

Dtrs,5:52 Exp,5:53-5:55 Cry,5:54-5:59 Dtrs,5:56
GCon,5:56 Drct,5:58-6:01 Pras,6:01 Cope,6:01-6:03 . . .

into the new timed event sequence

Dtrs,5:52 AAct,5:53-5:55 Cry,5:54-5:59 Dtrs,5:56
AAct,5:56 AAct,5:58-6:01 AAct,6:01 Cope,6:01-6:03 . . .

in which all adult acts are coded AAct.

The Recode command does not affect code boundaries or onset times, if relevant. For example, in the previous paragraph

Drct,5:58-6:01 Pras,6:01 . . .

was recoded to

AAct,5:58-6:01 AAct,6:01 . . .

not

AAct,5:58-6:02 . . .

thus preserving the boundaries that existed before recoding. Likewise, if codes A and B were recoded to a new code X, then the event sequence, A B A C A B, would become X X X C X X, and not X C X. Users who want successive events or states that are recoded to the same new code merged into one event (and not preserved as two successive identical events) should use the Lump command, as described in the next section.

Codes that are recoded to the same new code and that occupy the same time unit in timed event data, or the same interval in interval sequential data, are merged together. For example, again using Recode to recode adult behaviors from the child distress study (timed event sequences) into the AAct code, the sequence

Drct,5:58-6:21 Pras,6:01 Exp,6:08-6:12 GCon,6:15 . . .

would be recoded to

AAct,5:58- AAct,6:01- AAct,6:08- AAct,6:15-6:21 . . .

The time during which adult acts occurred is preserved as well as their separate onsets, but not the number of co-occurring separate acts nor the identities of the different acts. Similarly, using codes from the !Kung infant study (interval sequences),

RECODE IAct = IOfr IObj ISmi IVoc;

would change the interval sequence

IVoc XEnt *2, XOfr Rain+, IOfr IVoc ISmi, . . .

into the new interval sequence

IAct XEnt *2, XOfr Rain+, IAct, . . .

The Recode command preserves the fact that some infant activity occurred within an interval, but it does not preserve the number or separate identities of the different acts.

The Lump command

The Lump command is limited to event, state, and timed event sequences, although probably it would most often be used with event and state sequences. As noted in the previous paragraph, the Recode command may not always effect the desired changes in such sequences. *Autotransitions* – transitions from one code to itself, such as Alone Alone – are often not permitted within a set of mutually exclusive and exhaustive codes, whether events or states. If a user does not permit autotransitions in the data file and does not want any to result from recoding, then the Lump and not the Recode command should be used to modify data.

The general form for the Lump command is

LUMP *new_code* = *codes* ;

It recodes existing codes and at the same time lumps any sequences of codes with the same name together. The usual rules for naming new codes must be followed, and as many as 20 existing codes may be listed, in any order.

For example, the command

LUMP Move = Crawl Walk Run;

would change the event sequence

Quiet Run Walk Eat Crawl Walk Crawl Sleep . . .

into the new event sequence

Quiet Move Eat Move Sleep . . .

Similarly, using the state sequential example used previously,

LUMP Alone = Un Ob;

would change the state sequence

Un=2 Pe=3 Ob=1 Un=4 On=1 Ob=2 Un=5 . . .

into the new state sequence

Alone=2 Pe=3 Alone=5 On=1 Alone=7 . . .

This example demonstrates lumping within a single stream of states, but lumping within multiple streams of states works the same way.

One final example. Applied to the timed event sequence example used previously,

LUMP AAct = Exp Drct GCon Pras;

would change the timed event sequence

Drct,5:58-6:21 Pras,6:01 Exp,6:08-6:12 GCon,6:15 . . .

into the new timed event sequence

AAct,5:58-6:21 . . .

With timed event sequential data, Lump preserves only duration and not separate onsets. Users who desire duration only, for whatever reason, should use Lump instead of Recode; those who desire separate onsets to be preserved should use Recode, not Lump.

As a general rule, depending on whether autotransitions are allowed and what information the investigator wants to preserve and use, both Lump and Recode might be used with event and timed event sequential data. For example, it is often reasonable and meaningful to characterize two successive turns of talk with the same code, thus allowing auto-transitions in event sequences. Usually Lump and not Recode would be used with state sequential data. After all, if an identical state follows another, it is usually regarded as one ongoing state and not two successive ones. The Lump command, however, is not used with interval sequential data; lumping across intervals would violate the basic structure of the data and therefore specifying it for interval sequences results in a warning message and is ignored.

The Lump command has a further, rather specialized use. Sometimes it may be useful to merge any sequences of identical codes into a single code. This is accomplished with a single asterisk. Thus

LUMP * ;

indicates that any runs of identical codes are to be lumped together. Then identical successive events, states within a stream, and timed events (the onset for a code occurs in the next time unit after the offset of an identical code) are merged into one event, state, or timed event. Thus analysis of the transformed data would result in lower frequencies for these lumped codes. For example, the Lump command with an asterisk would change the event sequence

Quiet Run Run Walk Eat Crawl Walk Walk Walk Crawl Sleep

into the new event sequence

Quiet Run Walk Eat Crawl Walk Crawl Sleep

The Chain command

Sometimes it is desirable to assign a single name to a particular sequence or chain of codes. This can be done for event or interval sequences with the Chain command. If you want to name a particular sequence with SSD or TSD, first use the Event command (described later in this chapter) to transform such data into event sequences.

Used judiciously, the Chain command allows the investigation of three-event chains or even chains of greater length if desired. Its general form is

CHAIN *new_code = code_sequence* ;

It allows a chain or sequence of codes to be named. Whenever the exact sequence of codes defined to the right of the equals sign occurs, the entire sequence is treated as an occurrence of the new code defined to the left of the equals sign. Often the number of codes in the code sequence would be two, possibly three, and rarely more, although GSEQ permits up to 20. Unlike other data modification commands, the order of the codes is important for Chain; moreover, a code may appear more than once in the chain.

For example,

CHAIN Respond = Ask Answer;

would change the event sequence

Talk Answer Fuss Ask Talk Ask Answer Quiet . . .

into the new event sequence

Talk Answer Fuss Ask Talk Respond Quiet . . .

If Respond were defined as a target behavior, the investigator could now ask what behaviors precede responses (defining responses as Ask-Answer sequences), in effect investigating three-event sequences. Similarly,

CHAIN Cross = WCom HCom;

would change the event sequence

WEmp HNeg WCom HAp WCom HCom WEmo . . .

into the new event sequence

WEmp HNeg WCom HAp Cross WEmo . . .

If Cross were used as a given behavior, the investigator could now determine what behaviors follow, and if used as a target what behaviors precede, cross-complaining.

If the Chain command is used with interval sequential data, GSEQ searches for intervals that match the new sequence pattern and then replaces each code in the sequence with the new code, preserving interval boundaries. For example, the command

CHAIN IRecip = XOfr IOfr;

would change the interval sequence

IVoc XEnt *2, XOfr Rain +, IOfr IVoc ISmi, . . .

into the new interval sequence

IVoc XEnt *2, IRecip Rain+, IRecip IVoc ISmi, . . .

Frankly, we are not sure how many users will find the Chain command useful with interval sequential data. Far more often, we suspect, Chain will be used with event sequential data. Still, at least some investigators may find uses for Chain with ISD, so we have permitted it.

6.2 Removing codes

Under some circumstances it may be desirable to treat certain codes in a data file as though they were not there. This is done with the Remove command, whose general form is

REMOVE *codes* ;

It causes any of the named codes to be removed from consideration. They would not interrupt any sequences in which they are otherwise embedded or have any other effect on GSEQ. In particular, codes listed on the Remove command are not even considered by the data modification commands described in this chapter. As many as 20 codes may be listed, in any order.

GSEQ permits a maximum of 95 codes to be under consideration at any one time. This limit is intended to be generous, although you should understand that "under consideration" includes codes declared in the SDIS file (either explicitly or implicitly) as well as any new codes created using the commands described in this chapter and the next (although existing codes that are Recoded or Lumped are not counted because they are automatically removed after recoding or lumping). If the number of codes under consideration ever exceeds 95, you will need to remove some codes; otherwise GSEQ cannot proceed.

6.3 Creating codes for concurrent patterns

Concurrent codes occur with multiple state sequences, timed event sequences, and interval sequences that allow more than one code per interval. In such cases, new codes can be formed using standard logical operations effected with the And, Or, Not, Nor, and Xor commands. Their general forms are

AND *new_code = codes* ;
OR *new_code = codes* ;
NOT *new_code = codes* ;
NOR *new_code = codes* ;
XOR *new_code = codes* ;

As many as 20 codes may be listed, in any order.

For example, assume codes of A_talk, B_talk, C_talk, All_talk, Some_talk, Not_all, Silence, One_talk, and so forth. Then

AND All_talk = A_talk B_talk C_talk;

(the logical *and*) adds code All_talk to any time unit or interval in which A, B, and C all talked;

OR Some_talk = A_talk B_talk C_talk;

(the logical *or*) adds code Some_talk to any time unit or interval in which someone talked (whether just one, two, or all speakers);

NOT Not_all = A_talk B_talk C_talk;

(the negation of *and*) adds code Not_all to any time unit or interval in which A, B, and C did not all talk (perhaps no one talked, perhaps only one or two but not all three talked);

NOR Silence = A_talk B_talk C_talk;

(the negation of *or*) adds code Silence to any time unit or interval in which no one talked; and

XOR One_talk = A_talk B_talk C_talk;

(the exclusive *or*) adds code One_talk to any time unit or interval in which one, and only one, of the speakers (A, or B, or C) talked. Code One_talk is not added if more than one person talked or if no one talked.

6.4 Creating event sequences from state or other timed data

Occasionally it is useful to treat a single stream of states as event sequences, in effect ignoring duration. Lags then become event- instead of time-units for any subsequent analyses. In order to effect this transformation, simply specify

EVENT ;

No further information is required. The Event command makes no sense with interval sequences; such a request results in a warning message and is ignored. It may be requested for multiple state and timed event sequences, however, even though we think this would only occasionally be useful. Analysis of the transformed file would indicate how often the various codes were used, but if codes share the same onset time, an analysis of the order of codes might be misleading. Codes in the transformed file are ordered by their onset, but any codes that share the same onset time follow the default order for listing codes (see chapter 3), not the order of their occurrence in the original SDIS file.

Exactly which data types are appropriate for the various data modification commands are shown in Table 6.1.

Table 6.1. *Data types for which data modification commands are permitted.*

	Data Type				
Data Modification Command	Event (ESD)	State (SSD)	Multiple State (MSD)	Timed Event (TSD)	Interval (ISD)
RECODE	Yes	Yes	Yes	Yes	Yes
LUMP	Yes	Yes	Yes[a]	Yes	No
CHAIN	Yes	No	No	No	Yes
REMOVE	Yes	Yes	Yes	Yes	Yes
AND through XOR	No	No	Yes	Yes	Yes
EVENT	No	Yes	Yes	Yes	No
WINDOW	No	Yes	Yes	Yes	Yes

Note: The Window command is described in chapter 7.

[a] Permitted but rarely makes sense; use with caution.

6.5 Saving modified data

The modified version of the data may be saved for future use if you wish with the Save command. Its general form is

SAVE "*filename*" { OVERWRITE } ;

where *filename* follows standard DOS rules. It causes GSEQ to save the modified data in *filename*.MDS and its associated *filename*.DEF. Any extension supplied by the user is ignored. The DEF file contains code definitions and is automatically created by SDIS every time an MDS file is created (see Appendix A).

   If the file already exists, GSEQ will do nothing unless Overwrite is specified. In particular, GSEQ will not append a new MDS file to an existing one. If Overwrite is specified, GSEQ overwrites the existing MDS and DEF files, thereby destroying their previous versions. Subsequent File commands may then refer to the new files created by the Save command, in this or later runs.

6.6 Summary

In this chapter, we showed how to modify the data in an SDIS file for the duration of a GSEQ run and how to save it for future runs (see Tables 6.2 and 6.3). We demonstrated how to define new codes by recoding, lump-

Table 6.2. *GSEQ punctuation introduced in chapter 6.*

Mark	Interpretation
=	An equals sign separates the new code from existing codes for the Recode, Lump, And, Or, Not, Nor, and Xor commands and from the code sequence for the Chain command.
*	An asterisk on the Lump command indicates that all existing successive identical codes are to be lumped together.

Table 6.3. *GSEQ commands introduced in chapter 6.*

Command	Parameters
RECODE	*new_code = codes* ;
LUMP	[*new_code = codes* | *] ;
CHAIN	*new_code = code_sequence* ;
REMOVE	*codes* ;
AND	*new_code = codes* ;
OR	*new_code = codes* ;
NOT	*new_code = codes* ;
NOR	*new_code = codes* ;
XOR	*new_code = codes* ;
EVENT	;
SAVE	*"filename"* { OVERWRITE } ;

Note: A vertical line separates choices. Choices enclosed in braces are optional; choices enclosed in brackets are mandatory.

ing, and chaining old codes and by logically manipulating co-occurrences (and, or, not, etc.). In the next chapter we show how to define new codes that specify time windows, that is, periods of time keyed to the onsets and/or offsets of specific behaviors. These new codes provide considerable flexibility for the analysis of timed event sequences, in particular.

7
Specifying time windows

Topics covered in this chapter include:
1. A review of how existing codes are used to analyze lagged event and state sequences.
2. A review of how existing codes are used to analyze co-occurrences of state and timed events.
3. How to use the Window command to define new codes that specify periods of time keyed to onsets and/or offsets of existing codes.
4. How to use these new codes for analyzing primarily timed event data, and also multiple state and interval sequential data.

In previous chapters we have emphasized the importance of units of analysis, or tallying units – *events* for event sequences, *time units* for state and timed event sequences, or *intervals* for interval sequences. Especially when the unit is an event or interval, lags between units may play an important role. Like the metronome in music, lags tick off or segment the units coded. Hence lags typically are used only with event and interval data.

For state and timed event sequences, on the other hand, the time unit itself serves as the unit of analysis. In such cases, lags are rarely used. Instead, given and target codes are identified with the time period from the onset to the offset of a particular code (using existing codes as detailed in chapter 5 and revisited early in this chapter), or with other time periods keyed to the onsets or offsets of particular codes (defining new codes as described later in this chapter). Lags can be specified with state and timed event sequences, but because they are keyed to the time unit used, they typically slice the data too finely to be of much use.

In this chapter we show how new codes keyed to the onsets and offsets of existing codes can be defined using the Window command. These new codes define a period of time in an extremely flexible way and, like all codes, can be used on Target and Given commands. Usually these new codes would be used with TSD but they also work with SSD and ISD, as we demonstrate briefly in the final section of this chapter.

7.1 Review: Analyzing lagged event and state sequences

As described in chapter 5, given and target behaviors are identified with particular codes. These codes then serve as labels for the rows and columns of the contingency tables associated with each pair of Target and Given commands. The tallying unit for these tables, however, depends on the data type: events for event sequences, time units for state and timed events, and intervals for interval sequences. Consequently, the syntax introduced in chapter 5 is not only sufficient for lagged analyses of event and interval sequences, it is also sufficient for analyses of co-occurrences within state, timed event, and interval sequential data. Indeed, several examples of such analyses were presented in chapter 5.

By way of review, we begin this chapter with an ESD example. The following commands were applied to data from the infant attention study.

> FILE "*file_name*";
> EVENT;
> TARGET Un On Pe Ob Jt; LAG 1;
> GIVEN Un On Pe Ob Jt;

The commands request that GSEQ determine how often the five attentional states followed each other (lag 1). First, time information is removed from the initial state sequential data, leaving event sequences. The columns and rows of the resulting 5 × 5 table are labeled with the five attentional state codes. The form of the table looks like this:

GIVENS Lag 0	TARGETS, Lag 1				
	Un	On	Pe	Ob	Jt
Un					
On					
Pe					
Ob					
Jt					

The diagonal frequencies (the cells that go from the upper-left to the bottom-right corner of the table) would all be zero in this case because, by definition, these states are not allowed to follow themselves. In other words, these particular state codes cannot repeat, which has implications for some statistical computations, as described in chapter 8.

In contrast, the commands

> FILE "*file_name*";
> TARGET Un On Pe Ob Jt; LAG 1;
> GIVEN Un On Pe Ob Jt;

again request that GSEQ tally how often the five attentional states followed each other, and again the columns and rows of the resulting 5×5 table are labeled with the five attentional state codes. However, in this case successive time units (unlike successive events) can be coded identically. Thus, for example, the number of times adjacent seconds (assuming a time unit of a second) were both coded Unoccupied appears in the first column of the first row, the number of times an antecedent second was coded Unoccupied and the consequent second was coded Onlooking appears in the second column of the first row, and so forth.

The number of transitions between states would be the same for both the ESD and the SSD versions. Thus the off-diagonal cells for the two tables specified in the previous paragraphs would be identical; only their diagonal cells would differ. In the first case, the diagonal cells would be zero, and in the second, assuming that most states lasted for more than a few seconds, the tallies on the diagonal (which represent transitions from a state to the same state in the next second for SSD) might be quite large, probably larger than most of the off-diagonal cells (which represent transitions from one state to a different state).

Again, for both the ESD and SSD versions it would make no sense to specify a lag of zero. Both versions consist of a single stream of mutually exclusive and exhaustive events or states; consequently, all cells of the 5×5, lag 0 table would contain zero.

7.2 Analyzing co-occurrences of states and timed events

When more than one stream is coded, co-occurrences can be analyzed. Imagine that two streams were coded – one codes infants' state (Cry, Sleep, Alert), one infant's position (Supine, 45_degrees, Upright) – and that both coding schemes are mutually exclusive and exhaustive. Then the lag 0 specification

> TARGET Cry Sleep Alert;
> GIVEN Supine 45_degrees Upright;

makes sense. The resulting 3×3 table (rows labeled Supine, 45_degrees, Upright; columns labeled Cry, Sleep, Alert) looks like this:

GIVENS Lag 0	TARGETS, Lag 0		
	Cry	Sleep	Alert
Supine			
45_degrees			
Upright			

and indicates how many seconds the infant was both crying and supine, crying and held at a 45-degree angle, crying and upright, and so forth.

Co-occurrences for timed event sequences are specified in a similar way. For example, with codes from the child distress study and time recorded to the nearest second,

TARGET Cope &;
GIVEN Exp Dtct GCon Pras &;

requests that GSEQ form a 5×2 table. As described in chapter 5, the ampersand represents the residual category. Thus, the first row of the table divides the seconds coded Adult Explain into those that were also coded Child Cope and those that were not; the second row divides the seconds coded Adult Distract (that were not also coded Adult Explain; remember the hierarchy rule described in chapter 5) into those that were also coded Child Cope and those that were not; and so forth. The last row indicates the number of seconds coded Child Cope but none of the four adult behavior codes specified on the Given command (first cell) and the number of seconds coded neither Child Cope nor Adult Explain, Distract, Give Control, or Praise. The resulting table looks like this:

GIVENS Lag 0	TARGETS, Lag 0	
	Cope	&
Exp		
Dtct		
GCon		
Pras		
&		

Tallies of co-occurrences such as those just presented, which specify targets and givens using existing codes, may be sufficient for many investigations of state and timed event sequential data (and ISD as well). However, many users may find useful the more flexible time period–based syntax for new codes, as described in the next section.

7.3 Specifying time windows keyed to existing codes

The ability to specify targets and givens that represent not only times when a particular code occurs (using existing codes), but also *time periods* keyed to the onsets and/or offsets of particular codes (using new codes), gives GSEQ unique power and flexibility. Such new codes are specified with the Window command, whose general form is

> WINDOW *new_code* = *time_period* ;

Time periods (a stretch of adjacent time units or intervals) are primarily used with timed event sequential data but might also be used with multiple state and interval sequences.

For ease of exposition, the present discussion assumes a time unit of one second (as for the timed event sequences from the child distress study), but in practice the time unit is determined by the precision of times appearing in the SDIS data file (except for ISD files, for which the time unit is the interval). For example, if the user wants to define a code as all seconds coded for a particular behavior, then the time period is specified with the code itself, as demonstrated in the previous section. Thus

> TARGET Cry . . . ;

indicates that the first target consists of all seconds coded for child crying. In other words, the time period begins with the first second and continues through the last (inclusive) second coded for crying. Then the pair of commands,

> TARGET Cry &;
> GIVEN Drct &;

request that GSEQ determine the number of seconds coded for both child crying and adult distracting (Drct), for either, and for neither. For these examples, no new code is needed.

In general terms, the simplest form for expressing a time period, as exemplified in the last paragraph, is

> *code*

which specifies a time period coextensive with the code's duration. But that is exactly what an existing code does; in such cases, no new code is needed.

However, you might want to define a new code that is limited to the *onset unit* – the first time unit coded for the behavior – or the *offset unit* – the last time unit coded for the behavior (inclusive). In general terms, a left parenthesis preceding a code designates a period that includes only the onset time unit, whereas a right parenthesis following a code designates a period that includes only the offset time unit. Thus, if the time unit were a second, the onset second is indicated by

> (*code*

and the offset second by

> *code*)

Time periods can be stretched, both beyond and within the duration of a code, using plus and minus signs. Thus

> *code±n*
> (*code±n*
> *code*)±*n*

all indicate time periods that stretch an additional *n* time units (plus or minus, where *n* is no more than 100 absolute) and are anchored by all time units associated with a code, only its onset time, or only its (inclusive) offset time, respectively. For example,

> WINDOW CRY3 = Cry+3;

indicates a time period that includes all seconds coded for crying plus the three seconds after crying stops. Further examples are

> WINDOW CRYon2Af = (Cry+2;
> WINDOW CRYoff2Af = Cry)+2;
> WINDOW CRYon2B4 = (Cry-2;
> WINDOW CRYoff2B4 = Cry)-2;

All four of these examples indicate three-second time periods. The first begins with the onset of crying and continues for two more seconds (the window lasts three seconds no matter whether crying lasts one, two, three, or more seconds). The second begins with the last second for which crying was coded and continues for the next two seconds. The third begins two seconds before crying starts and terminates with the onset second for crying. And the fourth begins two seconds before crying stops and terminates with the offset second.

These four examples define time periods anchored to onsets or offsets. But occasionally it may be useful to define time periods not so anchored.

If two time periods are separated by a comma, GSEQ interprets the first as the beginning and the second as the ending (inclusive) of a time period. For example,

WINDOW CRY3B4 = (Cry-3,(Cry-1;

indicates a three-second time period that begins three seconds before and ends in the second just before the onset of crying, whereas

WINDOW Cry33 = Cry-3,Cry+3;

indicates a time period that begins three seconds before and ends three seconds after the crying bout. If two specifications are used, the first must occur before the second, of course; anything else is an error. These and other time period specifications are depicted in Figure 7.1. If you understand Figure 7.1, you will understand how to specify time periods keyed to onsets, offsets, or durations of particular behaviors.

The Window command can be used to answer relatively complex questions such as how often an infant began crying within 10 seconds of the time an adult began distracting. For example, GSEQ would give this tally if you specified

WINDOW Cry_Onset = (Cry;
WINDOW Drct_On10 = (Drct+9;
TARGET Cry_Onset &;
GIVEN Drct_On10 &;

Truncated and null windows (advanced topic)

The Window command is remarkably flexible. The windows it specifies are affected by the timing of the codes already in the file, and occasionally this very flexibility can result in anomalies. Some windows may extend before the beginning or after the end of a session, in which case they are truncated. Others may overlap, in which case the later windows are truncated. Still others may be null (i.e., have no duration). Examples are given in the next paragraphs, but in any case GSEQ lists the number of truncated and null windows and the number that overlapped.

Consider the following 10-second session:

Timed; ,1 Cry,3-8 ,11/

Then if you specified

WINDOW CRYon5B4 = (Cry-5;
WINDOW CRYoff5Af = Cry)+5;

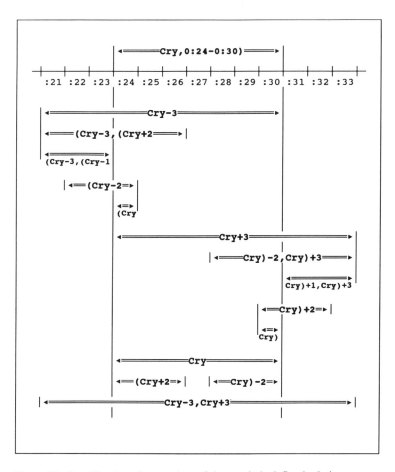

Figure 7.1. Specifications for a variety of time periods defined relative to a bout of crying. For this example, "Cry, 0:24-0:30)" represents the crying bout in the SDIS file. In contrast, "Cry-3," "(Cry-3,(Cry+2," and so forth, represent time windows to GSEQ (with "Cry" representing the entire bout). Keeping this in mind, the different forms and purposes of SDIS and GSEQ syntax should not confuse you. As usual, the first interval marked represents time 0:21, the second 0:22, and so forth.

both windows would be truncated, the first to the first three seconds and the second to the last four seconds of the session. Windows can also be truncated by another window. Consider this session fragment:

    ... Cry,11 Cry,14-23 ...

Then

WINDOW CRYon4af = (Cry+4;

would identify two five-second windows, but they would overlap in seconds 14 and 15. GSEQ gives priority to the first window, which extends from seconds 11 to 15 inclusive. Therefore the second window would be truncated, so instead of extending from second 14, it would extend from seconds 16 to 18 inclusive.

Not all possible window specifications are listed in Figure 7.1. For example,

WINDOW Cry_middle = (Cry+2,Cry)-2;

indicates a time window that begins in the second time unit after the onset and ends in the second time unit before the offset window. The duration of windows identified by this specification depends on the length of the cry bout, and for short bouts could have no duration at all. For example, if a cry bout lasted four time units or less, the window would be null. In any event, as noted earlier, GSEQ displays the number of null windows, if any.

7.4 Using time periods with interval sequences

The syntax for time periods described in the previous section is often used with state and timed event sequential data, but it can be used quite productively with interval sequential data as well, in which case the interval defines the time unit. For example,

WINDOW IVoc_On = (IVoc;

specifies a new code that occurs only in the onset interval for infant vocalizing (i.e., the first in a series of intervals coded for infant vocalization), not in all intervals so coded. Thus

WINDOW XVoc_On = (XVoc;
TARGET IVoc_On;
LAG 0 1 2;
GIVEN XVoc_On;

requests that GSEQ determine how often, given that another person began vocalizing to the infant in one interval, the infant began vocalizing in the same interval (lag 0), or in the following interval (lag 1), or after one intervening interval (lag 2), where began or onset is defined as an interval coded for a behavior that is not preceded by an interval also coded for that behavior. Similarly,

WINDOW IVoc_Off = IVoc);
TARGET XVoc_On;

LAG 1;
GIVEN IVoc_Off;

requests that GSEQ determine how often another person began vocalizing in an interval immediately after (i.e., at lag 1) an interval coded for the offset of infant vocalizing, where *offset* is defined as an interval coded for a behavior that is not followed by an interval also coded for that behavior.

Givens and targets can also include several intervals in succession. For example,

WINDOW XVoc_On2 = (XVoc+2;
TARGET IVoc_On;
GIVEN XVoc_On2;

requests that GSEQ determine how often an infant began vocalizing in any interval coded for the onset, or within two intervals of the onset, of another person vocalizing to the infant. Note that this last example, which did not specify any lags, provides quite different information from the example in the previous paragraph that requested lags 0, 1, and 2. Similarly,

WINDOW IOfr1 = IOfr+1;
TARGET XOfr;
GIVEN IOfr1;

requests that GSEQ determine how often Other Offered was coded, either in the same interval as one coded for Infant Offering or in the immediately following interval.

Under most circumstances, the time period syntax exemplified in Figure 7.1 (with the exception of syntax specifying onset and offset intervals) would be used with interval sequential data to specify givens, not targets. This allows investigators to ask how often certain events occur in a particular context, that is, how often targets – all intervals or just onset or offset intervals coded for a behavior – occur relative to a given behavioral context, which can be flexibly defined as a stretch of intervals using all the forms shown in Figure 7.1.

Just as the ampersand is often used with state or timed event sequences to ensure an exhaustive tallying of all time units, the ampersand also is used to ensure an exhaustive tallying of all intervals. For example,

WINDOW IOfr1 = IOfr+1;
TARGET XOfr &;
GIVEN IOfr1 &;

requests that GSEQ form a 2 × 2 table. If an interval is coded Infant Offers, or if an interval follows one that is, that interval is tallied in row

1; all other intervals are tallied in row 2. And if that interval is coded Other Offers, the tally is added to column 1, otherwise to column 2. As noted earlier and again in the next section, without such exhaustive tallying, contingency table statistics other than joint frequencies are difficult or impossible to interpret.

7.5 Hierarchical processing revisited

No matter whether the tallying units are events, time units, or intervals, each unit is permitted to add a tally to one, and only one, cell of the contingency table under consideration. This assures a mutually exclusive allocation of tallies to the table. Such an allocation is basic to the definition of a contingency table and, for that reason, is enforced by GSEQ with its hierarchical rule (codes appearing earlier in the list are given preference, as described in chapter 5).

In addition, exhaustive contingency tables are amenable to statistical analysis and interpretation in a way that nonexhaustive tables are not, which makes the residual code (signified with an ampersand, as described in chapter 5) very useful. Whenever data consist of a single stream of ME&E codes, and only some of those codes are listed on the Target and Given commands, it will almost always make sense to complete the list of codes with an ampersand.

The residual code is also useful when codes can co-occur, as is true for multiple streams of state sequences, most timed event sequences, and for interval sequences that permit more than one code per interval. In such cases, judicious choices of time periods coupled with the residual code ensure that the rows and columns of the contingency table are labeled with meaningful, mutually exclusive and exhaustive specifications of target and given behaviors. Several examples of such use have been presented, in this as well as previous chapters. Indeed, when analyzing timed event sequences or any data that permit co-occurring codes, probably the ampersand will appear on Target and Given commands far more often than not. In fact, we considered making it a default, but thought it clearer if a specification for each row and column of the contingency table, including the residual one, were explicitly listed on Target and Given commands.

7.6 Summary

This chapter completes the presentation of GSEQ's data modifications (see Tables 7.1 and 7.2). Chapter 5 showed how to specify targets and

Table 7.1. *GSEQ punctuation introduced in chapter 7.*

Mark	Interpretation
(	A left parenthesis before a code indicates its onset time unit or interval.
)	A right parenthesis after a code indicates its inclusive offset time unit or interval.
+	A plus sign after a specification and before a number indicates a forward extension of time units or intervals.
-	A hyphen or minus sign after a specification and before a number indicates a backward extension of time units or intervals.
,	Commas between two specifications separate the beginning and ending of a time period or a stretch of intervals.

Table 7.2. *GSEQ command introduced in chapter 7.*

Command	Parameters
WINDOW	*new_code = time_period* ;

givens using existing codes. Chapter 6 demonstrated how to form new codes from existing ones using Recode, Lump, and other data modification commands. This chapter presented how to define new codes that represent time periods (several adjacent time units or intervals) keyed to onsets and/or offsets of particular behaviors. The rows and columns of the tables GSEQ produces are defined by codes; these codes may be ones defined initially in the SDIS data file or formed from them using any of a number of data modification commands, including the Window command introduced in this chapter.

As has been shown, the tallying unit depends on the type of data analyzed, and the cells of the two-dimensional contingency tables GSEQ produces contain joint frequencies, expressed in the appropriate units (events, time units, or intervals). The hierarchical rule and the use of the residual category are important when the appropriate units are tallied. The next chapter presents the various statistics, in addition to joint frequencies, that GSEQ computes based on the two-dimensional tables defined by the Target and Given commands.

8

Computing contingency table statistics with GSEQ

Topics covered in this chapter include:

1. The contingency table statistics GSEQ computes and how the Stats command can be used to request them.
2. The computational adjustments GSEQ makes when adjacent events cannot repeat (i.e., cannot both be assigned the same code).
3. How the Variables command can be used to provide names (or labels) for any design variables and levels of design variables.
4. How the Pool command can be used to pool tallies over subjects, or over levels of a variable, prior to computing statistics.
5. The simple or unconditional statistics GSEQ computes and how the Simple command can be used to request them.
6. How to export the tables produced by GSEQ for subsequent log-linear analyses using BMDP, ILOG, or SPSS.

Chapters 5, 6, and 7 showed how to specify the rows and columns of two-dimensional contingency tables using the Target, Given, and Lag commands. Labels for the rows and columns could be simple code names, designated periods of time (or stretches of intervals) keyed to onsets and offsets of particular codes (using the Window command), or the residual code (i.e., the ampersand); the tallying unit or unit of analysis could be an event, a time unit, or an interval. In any case, GSEQ first determines the number of tallies for each cell in the tables specified. Then, based on further specifications you provide, GSEQ produces the results of a number of different possible computations based on those tallies. We are finally nearing our goal: descriptive statistics derived from the sequential data, which presumably justify all our efforts so far.

Recall that data for what we call a *subject* is terminated with a slash in the SDIS data file. By default, GSEQ produces at least one table per subject for each Target command in the GSEQ command file (more may be produced if lags are specified). In this chapter we describe the computations included in GSEQ, explain how the user specifies them, and explain how the default of one table per subject for each Target command (for each lag specified) can be modified using the Pool command.

8.1 Specifying statistics with the Stats command

GSEQ is capable of deriving a number of different statistics from the contingency tables you request. The ones desired for a particular analysis are specified with the Stats command, whose general form is

STATS *stat_specs* ;

The Stats command must precede (not follow) the Target and Given commands to which it applies. Most statistical specifications are three- or four-letter abbreviations, and any number of them in any order may be included in a single Stats command, or ALL may be specified, in which case all statistics suitable for a given table are computed. Like the Title command and the data modification commands, the Stats command applies to the table or tables produced by the following Target command, and to all tables produced thereafter by subsequent Target commands until another Stats command (if any) is encountered. If an additional Stats command is encountered, the new specifications replace the old ones. If no Stats command appears before a Target command, only joint frequencies are displayed.

Cell statistics

Several statistics (observed and expected frequencies, raw and adjusted residuals, and conditional probabilities) are computed for each cell in the table. These cell statistics are described in the following paragraphs. Note that, with the exception of observed frequencies, these statistics make sense only when target and given behaviors are defined so that a coherent sample of behavior is exhaustively tallied. Here and elsewhere, GSEQ will mindlessly compute whatever you request. But it remains your responsibility to make sure that the requests make sense.

Observed joint frequencies are specified by the abbreviation JNTF. Joint frequencies are tallied for all cells by default; thus it is not necessary to include JNTF in the list of statistical specifications. If for some reason you do not want joint frequencies included in the output, specify NOJF.

Expected joint frequencies are specified by the abbreviation EXPF. The expected joint frequency for the cell located at the intersection of row r of the givens and column c of the targets is defined as

$$expf(r,c) = p(c)\,f(r) \tag{8.1}$$

where $f(r)$ is the total frequency observed for row r. This can also be written

$$m_{ij} = p_{+j}\, x_{i+} \tag{8.2}$$

where m is an expected frequency and x is an observed frequency. The subscripts i and j refer to row and column positions, respectively, and the plus sign indicates summation so that x_{i+} indicates the sum for row i. The overall probability for the code in column c – designated $p(c)$ – is estimated as $f(c)$ divided by N, the total number of tallies. Thus, equations (8.1) and (8.2) can also be written in either of two quite different notations, as follows.

$$expf(r,c) = \frac{f(c)}{N}\, f(r) = \frac{f(c)\, f(r)}{N} \tag{8.3}$$

and

$$m_{ij} = \frac{x_{+j}}{x_{++}}\, x_{i+} = \frac{x_{+j}\, x_{i+}}{x_{++}} \tag{8.4}$$

Some readers may prefer the more informal style of equations (8.1) and (8.3) whereas others may prefer the more formal but also more conventional style of equations (8.2) and (8.4). In any case, these equations for expected frequencies assume no constraints such as those imposed when adjacent codes cannot repeat, as discussed in the next section.

Raw residuals are specified by the abbreviation RSDL. The raw residual for the cell located at the intersection of row r and column c is defined as

$$res(r,c) = f(r,c) - expf(r,c) \tag{8.5}$$

or

$$d_{ij} = x_{ij} - m_{ij} \tag{8.6}$$

where d (for difference) represents a raw residual. Raw residuals are used in the standard definition for the Pearson chi-square but because their interpretation depends, in part, on the number of tallies in an individual table, they are not very useful for making cross-table comparisons.

Adjusted residuals are specified by the abbreviation ADJR; they are standardized versions of the raw residuals. The adjusted residual for the cell located at the intersection of row r and column c is defined as

$$z(r,c) = \frac{f(r,c) - expf(r,c)}{\sqrt{expf(r,c)\, [1 - p(c)]\, [1 - p(r)]}} \tag{8.7}$$

or

$$z_{ij} = \frac{x_{ij} - m_{ij}}{\sqrt{m_{ij}\,(1 - p_{+j})\,(1 - p_{i+})}} \tag{8.8}$$

(Haberman, 1978). A similar but not identical version of equation (8.8) appears in an article by Allison and Liker (1982), thus this statistic is sometimes called the Allison and Liker z score in the sequential analysis literature (see Bakeman & Gottman, 1986, pp. 154–155; Bakeman & Quera, submitted). Adjusted residuals are distributed approximately normally, assuming independence of tallies, and the approximation becomes better as x_{i+} increases. When GSEQ detects conditions that call normality into question (e.g., $m_{ij}/x_{i+} > .9$ or $< .1$ or $x_{i+} < 30$), a warning message is issued; still, the absence of a warning message should not be taken as a guarantee of normality.

Equation (8.8) provides a better approximation than another statistic often used in log-linear texts and programs. Called the *standardized residual*, it is defined as

$$s(r,c) = \frac{f(r,c) - expf(r,c)}{\sqrt{expf(r,c)}} \tag{8.9}$$

or

$$s_{ij} = \frac{x_{ij} - m_{ij}}{\sqrt{m_{ij}}} \tag{8.10}$$

(Haberman, 1979). Equations (8.9) and (8.10) can always be used to compute a standardized residual, whereas equations (8.7) and (8.8) – like equations (8.1)–(8.4) – assume the absence of constraints such as those imposed by codes that cannot repeat.

Conditional probabilities are specified with the abbreviation CONP. These are estimates of probabilities for target behaviors, not overall, but in conjunction with specified given behaviors. The conditional (or transitional) probability for the cell located at the intersection of row r of the givens and column c of the targets is defined as

$$p(c|r) = \frac{f(r,c)}{f(r)} \tag{8.11}$$

where the vertical bar is read *given* (hence, the probability of c given r), or

$$p_{j|i} = \frac{x_{ij}}{x_{i+}} \tag{8.12}$$

By definition, all conditional probabilities in a row sum to one.

Table statistics

Other statistics are computed, not for each cell in the table, but for the table overall (Pearson and likelihood-ratio chi-square, and kappa). These statistics are described in the following paragraphs. As with expected frequencies and other cell statistics, GSEQ will compute a number based on whatever tallies appear in the tables. But these statistics make sense only when target and given behaviors are exhaustively defined, and it is your responsibility to make sure they are.

The *Pearson chi-square* is specified by the abbreviation XSQ. The computed chi-square is symbolized here as X^2 (Roman letter), thus reserving the Greek letter chi for the theoretical chi-square distribution. Unlike the residuals and adjusted residuals, which are computed for each cell in a table, chi-square is computed for the entire table. Most readers are probably familiar with this common statistic. It is defined as

$$X^2 = \sum \frac{[f(r,c) - expf(r,c)]^2}{expf(r,c)} \tag{8.13}$$

or

$$X^2 = \sum \frac{(x_{ij} - m_{ij})^2}{m_{ij}} \tag{8.14}$$

summed over all cells with nonzero m_{ij}. Usually in the context of a two-dimensional table, chi-square is used to determine whether the row factor is significantly associated with the column factor, granted certain assumptions such as independence of tallies. For a given degree of association, the value of chi-square increases with the sample size, thus chi-square does not assess the degree of association (i.e., the magnitude of the effect) very well.

The *likelihood-ratio chi-square* is specified by the abbreviation GSQ, usually symbolized as G^2. It is defined as

$$G^2 = 2 \sum f(r,c) \ [\log_e f(r,c) - \log_e expf(r,c)] \tag{8.15}$$

or

$$G^2 = 2 \sum x_{ij} \ (\log_e x_{ij} - \log_e m_{ij}) \tag{8.16}$$

summed over all cells with nonzero x_{ij} and m_{ij}, where $\log_e$ stands for the natural logarithm. Both X^2 and G^2 are distributed approximately as chi-square, and generally will give similar values for the same table, but for technical reasons (which matter primarily for higher-order tables) G^2 is often preferred for log-linear analyses (see Fienberg, 1980). Compared to

G^2, however, the approximation provided by X^2 is somewhat more robust for small samples (see Wickens, 1989, p. 38).

Cohen's (1960) *kappa*, which often is used as an index of agreement, is specified by the abbreviation KAPPA. It is defined as

$$k = \frac{P_{obs} - P_{exp}}{1 - P_{exp}}$$ (8.17)

P_{obs} is the proportion of agreement observed. It is the sum of the tallies on the diagonal divided by the total number of tallies, or

$$P_{obs} = \frac{\sum x_{ii}}{N} \ (i = 1 \text{ to } K)$$

where $N = x_{++}$ and K is the order of the matrix (i.e., the number of codes; remember, for kappa the number of rows and columns are the same). P_{exp} is the proportion of agreement expected due to chance. It is the sum of the products of row by column sums divided by N squared, or

$$P_{exp} = \frac{\sum x_{+i} x_{i+}}{N^2} \ (i = 1 \text{ to } K)$$

where one row sum by column sum cross product is computed for each diagonal cell.

GSEQ will compute a value for kappa as long as the table is square. However, you should make certain that the given codes derive from one observer and the target codes from another, that otherwise target and given codes refer to the same behavior and are listed in the same order, and that data are concurrent (i.e., lag 0). Otherwise kappa cannot be interpreted as a measure of agreement. (Other interpretations are possible, of course. At lags other than 0, e.g., kappa could be interpreted as some sort of measure of self-transition.)

Statistics for 2 × 2 tables

Some table statistics make sense only for 2 × 2 tables, which have a number of unique properties (e.g., the absolute values of the residuals and the adjusted residuals are the same for all four cells, and the value of the adjusted residual is the same as the square root of the Pearson chisquare). GSEQ computes two of these: the odds ratio and Yule's Q.

The *odds ratio*, a statistic commonly used in epidemiology but less frequently in psychology, is specified by the abbreviation ODDS. It is especially appropriate when rows represent different samples, such as husbands and wives, and columns represent the presence or absence of a particular behavior. Unlike chi-square, it is not affected by the sample size, and so is often used to index the magnitude of the effect. If *a*, *b*, *c*, and *d* represent the four cells of a 2×2 table as follows:

	B	Not-B
A	*a*	*b*
Not-A	*c*	*d*

then the odds ratio is defined as

$$odds\ ratio = \frac{a/b}{c/d} \tag{8.18}$$

The odds ratio ranges from zero for a perfect negative relation, to one for no relation, to positive infinity for a perfect positive relation.

Yule's Q is specified by the abbreviation YULQ. Users who are uneasy with an index such as the odds ratio, which varies from zero to one to infinity, may prefer Yule's Q, which is a variant of the odds ratio. Using the definitions for *a*, *b*, *c*, and *d* given previously, Yule's Q is defined as

$$Yule's\ Q = \frac{ad - bc}{ad + bc} \tag{8.19}$$

Yule's Q ranges from minus one for a perfect negative relation, to zero for no relation, to plus one for a perfect positive relation, making it analogous to the familiar correlation coefficient. This and other statistical specifications for the Stats command are summarized in Table 8.1.

Concerning statistical significance

As noted earlier, granted certain assumptions, adjusted residuals are distributed approximately normally, so many users will refer to adjusted residuals greater than 1.96 absolute as significant at the .05 level. Similarly, X^2 and G^2, again granted certain assumptions, are distributed approximately as chi-square with $(r - 1)(c - 1)$ degrees of freedom, and so again many users will refer to statistics that exceed their appropriate critical values as statistically significant.

An interpretation of statistical significance that is too literal is not always wise. In the course of a single analysis many tests of significance may be made, and some may be significant just by chance (type I errors). As a result, some authorities suggest applying the Bonferroni correction:

Table 8.1. *Stats command: Statistical specifications.*

Spec	Interpretation
ALL	All cell and table statistics that apply
	Cell Statistics
JNTF	Observed joint frequencies (the default)
EXPF	Expected joint frequencies
RSDL	Raw residuals
ADJR	Adjusted residuals
CONP	Conditional probabilities
NOJF	No joint frequencies (reverses default)
	Table Statistics
XSQ	Pearson chi-square
GSQ	Likelihood-ratio chi-square
KAPPA	Cohen's kappa
ODDS	Odds ratio
YULQ	Yule's Q

instead of .05, .05 divided by the number of tests is used as the alpha level, which has the effect of imposing a study-wise alpha level of .05.

Occasionally, users of sequential analysis make a few specific predictions and then attempt to confirm them, in which case type I error is not generally a problem. Far more frequently, however, sequential analysis is used in exploratory work for which type I error can be a serious consideration. The Bonferroni correction offers some protection, but no matter what alpha level is used, significant results within tables (i.e., significant residuals) should probably be ignored unless the chi-square associated with the particular table is significant (Bakeman & Quera, submitted). The chi-square is like an omnibus analysis of variance test and a significant result is like a permit, giving us license to explore further.

Remember, too, that a particular X^2 or G^2 is distributed only approximately as chi-square, and that the approximation becomes better the greater the number of tallies. If the number of tallies in a table is small, you should regard the apparent significance level with some skepticism. A common rule of thumb suggests that there should be at least five times more tallies than cells, and at least 80% of the cells should have expected (not observed) frequencies of 5 or higher (Tabachnick & Fidell, 1989; Wickens, 1989). To give a sense of how many expected frequencies are small, GSEQ displays the percent of cells whose expected frequencies are less than 5, 3, and 1.

Further, some writers (e.g, Faraone & Dorfman, 1987; cf. Bakeman & Dorval, 1989) question whether assumptions required for significance testing can ever be met by sequential data. They recommend robust tests such as the jackknife for significance testing. Such tests are appealing but extremely computation intensive. Given the general exploratory and descriptive thrust of GSEQ, we have not included them here but encourage interested readers to pursue the matter, especially in the presence of one or two strong and theoretically important predictions.

8.2 Adjustments for codes that cannot repeat

Under most circumstances, expected frequencies for two-dimensional tables can be computed using equation (8.4), which we call MM, or the marginal model, because it relies on totals in the margins. An important exception occurs when, usually for logical or definitional reasons, successive events cannot both be assigned the same code. Then, when event sequences are analyzed and lags 1 or greater are under consideration, computational adjustments are required. The discussion in this section applies to such cases. (Incidentally, all comments made in this section refer to absolute lags; thus, comments concerning lag 1 also apply to lag −1, and comments concerning lags greater than 1 also apply to lags less than −1.)

You may skip this section if you do not have ESD or if you have ESD but successive events may be assigned the same code. However, if nonrepeatability characterizes your codes, you should set the SDIS option *repeat code check* to *yes* when processing your SDS file initially (see chapter 9). Then any codes that accidentally repeat will be flagged as errors and, more to the point for present purposes, GSEQ will know that your file consists of nonrepeating events and will adjust computations accordingly.

Lag 1

Consider lag 1 first. If adjacent events cannot be assigned the same code, then all auto-transitions (e.g., code A at lag 0 to code A at lag 1) must be zero. Such zeros are called logical zeros, or *structural zeros*, to distinguish them from transitions that just happen to be zero in a particular sample (*empirical zeros*). Structural zeros affect the values computed for expected frequencies and, because expected frequencies are used to compute residuals, adjusted residuals, and chi-squares, affect the values computed for these last three statistics as well.

A number of formulas for lag 1 expected frequencies when adjacent events cannot repeat have been proposed in the literature (for a review, see Bakeman & Quera, submitted). For example, Sackett (1979) proposed:

$$expf(t_1|g_0) = \frac{f(t)}{N - f(g)} f(g)$$

(8.20)

where t represents the column or target, g is the row or given, and subscripts 1 and 0 indicate lags. This can also be rewritten:

$$m_{ij} = \frac{x_{+j}}{x_{++} - x_{i+}} x_{i+}$$

(8.21)

But all such formulas share a common problem: the row and column totals for the expected frequencies fail to match the observed ones as they should. The correct solution was noted by Lemon and Chatfield (1971; see also Van Hooff, 1982), who wrote that any closed-form formula was only approximate and that an exact solution requires an iterative procedure, as proposed by Goodman (1968). Such a procedure (the Deming-Stephan algorithm, also called IPF, or Iterative Proportional Fitting) is used by GSEQ to compute lag 1 expected frequencies in the presence of structural zeros.

Under most circumstances, GSEQ computes expected frequencies according to MM (equation (8.4)). However, if SDIS's repeat code check was set to *yes*, data are event sequences, and target and given lists contain the same K codes, then any lag 1 autotransitions are assumed to be structurally zero and IPF is used to compute expected frequencies. If chi-squares are requested, degrees of freedom are adjusted accordingly. For example, usually degrees of freedom (df) for a $K \times K$ table are $(K - 1)^2$; with structural zeros on the diagonal, they are $(K - 1)^2 - K$ instead (in general, the df are reduced by the number of structural zeros).

Given structural zeros, a number of ways of computing adjusted residuals are proposed in the literature (see, e.g., Bishop, Fienberg, & Holland, 1975; Haberman, 1978). One of the better approximations is defined by Haberman (1978), but it relies on extremely complex computations which require a Newton-Raphson fitting algorithm (it is computed by LOGLINEAR in SPSS). One of the easiest to compute is given in equation (8.10) (standardized residual), but it gives quite conservative results (it is computed by HILOGLINEAR in SPSS). Equation (8.8), as defined by Haberman, applies to tables without structural zeros, and is also given in the lag-sequential literature (Sackett, 1979).

GSEQ always uses equation (8.8) (i.e., the Allison & Liker z) to compute adjusted residuals. Absent structural zeros, it is correct. Moreover, given structural zeros, our simulation studies indicate that it is a reasonable approximation and, if anything, is overly conservative, especially when there are few codes, but not so severely conservative as equation (8.10) (Bakeman & Quera, submitted).

The Zeros command (advanced topic)

The procedure just described permits only autotransitions to be structurally zero. Occasionally a sophisticated user may wish to control exactly which lag 1 transitions are structurally zero. This can be done with the Zeros command, whose general form is

ZEROS (*row1*, *col1*) { (*row2*, *col2*) } . . . ;

Pairs of numbers are specified. The first is a row index and the second a column index. Together they identify a cell that is to be treated as structurally zero. The punctuation is optional; that is, the parentheses and commas, included here for readability, may be omitted. No more than 20 pairs may be specified, and the indices must be greater than 0 and less than or equal to 20.

If used at all, the Zeros command must directly follow a Stats command, and affects all subsequent Target-Given tables until a new Stats command is encountered. Only lag 1 computations are affected (not lag −1). Expected frequencies are computed with IPF, but only the cells declared on the Zeros command, and no others, are treated as structural zeros. ZEROS may be requested for any data type and for tables of any size. Degrees of freedom are $(r - 1)(c - 1) - k$, where r is the number of rows, c is the number of columns, and k is the number of structural zeros. Expected frequencies, and so other statistics based on them, are affected by the Zeros command. Clearly, it should be used with some caution and a firm understanding of log-linear analysis (see, e.g., Wickens, 1989).

Lags greater than 1

The effect of codes that cannot repeat extends beyond lag 1, but no way of computing expected frequencies at greater lags seems quite as tidy as the lag 1 method. Let L indicate the lag under consideration and **0L** a table, produced by the Lag command, whose rows and columns represent lag 0 and L, respectively. For now, assume that L is always greater than 1. (Any comments concerning lags greater than 1 in this section apply equally to lags less than −1.) Assume also that data are ESD and that Target and Given lists contain the same codes. A moment's reflection shows that MM (equation (8.4)) does not yield reasonable expected frequencies. For example, if all codes were equiprobable, then at lag 2 expected frequencies on the diagonal should be greater than those off it (and the reverse at lag 3), yet equation (8.4) would result in uniform transitional probabilities throughout.

Two methods for computing expected frequencies at lags greater than 1 when codes cannot repeat have been suggested. Sackett (1979) recommended

$$expf(t_L|g_0) = \frac{f(t) - f(t_{L-1}|g_0)}{N - f(g)} f(g)$$

(8.22)

where t represents the column (or target), g the row (or given), and L the lag. Thus $f(t_{L-1}|g_0)$ indicates the number of times after a particular given behavior at lag 0 the target behavior occurred at lag $L-1$. We have rewritten this as

$$m_{ij} = \frac{x_{+j} - y_{ij}}{x_{++} - y_{i+}} x_{i+}$$

(8.23)

where x and y refer to cells in the lag 0–lag L and lag 0–lag $L-1$ tables, respectively. A rationale for this computation is presented in Sackett (1979) and Bakeman and Quera (submitted). We refer to equation (8.23) as GS, after Sackett.

Additionally, we have proposed

$$m_{ij} = t_{ij} x_{i+}$$

(8.24)

where t is an element in a matrix of expected lag 0–lag L transitional probabilities, $\mathbf{0L}_{TP}$. This matrix is produced by multiplying together two matrices of observed transitional probabilities. Symbolically, this is

$$\mathbf{0L}_{TP} = \mathbf{0M}_{TP} \; \mathbf{ML}_{TP}$$

(8.25)

Rows and columns for the $\mathbf{0M}_{TP}$ matrix represent lag 0 and lag $L-1$ (represented with M for minus), whereas rows and columns for the $\mathbf{ML}_{TP}$ matrix represent lag $L-1$ and lag L. We call this the CK procedure because equation (8.25) is the matrix form for what is known as the Chapman-Kolmogorov equation (see, e.g., Wickens, 1982). (To multiply these two matrices, given and target codes must be the same and must be in the same order; if they are specified in a different order, GSEQ sorts them so that the multiplication can be done.) A rationale for this computation based on log-linear analytic considerations is presented in Bakeman and Quera (submitted), and our simulation studies therein suggest that GS (equation (8.23)) performs somewhat better than CK (equation (8.24)), given the sort of overlapped tallying that is standard in sequential analysis and that GSEQ performs.

Thus, if SDIS's repeat code check is set to *yes*, data are event sequences, and target and given lists contain the same K codes, then GS (equation (8.23)) is used to compute any lag 2 or greater expected frequencies. If chi-squares are requested, degrees of freedom are $(K - 1)^2 - 1$, not the $(K - 1)^2$ that might be expected (they are the same for CK except when the lag is 2, then they are $(K - 1)^2 - 2$). As noted earlier, adjusted residuals, here as elsewhere, are computed according to equation (8.8). Finally, it goes without saying that given and target lists should make conceptual sense, but that, as always, is your responsibility.

Changing default computations

Occasionally you may wish to alter the default computations (e.g., to use equation (8.24) not (8.23) at lags greater than 1). These desires, like cell and table statistics, are represented by simple abbreviations. If expressed, they are enclosed in parentheses and follow the list of statistics requested. Thus the expanded general form for the Stats command is

STATS *stat_specs* { *(options)* } ;

Permitted options are MREP (for may repeat), NREP (for cannot repeat), NRCK (for cannot repeat, CK or Chapman-Kolmogorov procedure), and TEST (which is the default). The effect of these options is detailed in Table 8.2. No more than one option may be specified. They affect computations only when data are ESD; for non-ESD data, GSEQ always proceeds as if MREP had been specified, no matter the actual option.

8.3 Labeling variables and levels of variables

Conventions for SDIS data files, as detailed in chapter 3, allow for the inclusion of design information. A subject (dyad, family, etc.) may be represented with data from one or more observation sessions. Data from several subjects may be present, and subjects may be assigned to various levels of several different factors or variables. Recall that, if the design includes only one factor, data for subjects assigned to the first level of that factor end with (1), to the second level end with (2), and so forth, whereas if the design includes two factors, data for subjects assigned to the first level of the first factor and the third level of the second factor end with (1,3), and so forth.

Thus, in the SDIS data file, cells in the design (not to be confused with cells in the contingency table) are indicated by lists of numbers enclosed in parentheses. Variables are indicated by position in the list, and levels

Table 8.2. *Stats command: Computing options.*

Option	Interpretation
MREP	Even if the repeat code check option was *yes*, compute all expected frequencies at all lags using MM (equation (8.4)); no transitions are regarded as structurally zero.
NREP	Even if the repeat code check option was *no* (and assuming ESD and the same codes on both target and given lists), at lag 1 absolute regard all autotransitions as structurally zero and compute expected frequencies with IPF. At lags greater than 1 absolute compute expected frequencies using GS (equation (8.23)).
NRCK	Even if the repeat code check option was *no* (and assuming ESD and the same codes on both target and given lists), at lag 1 absolute regard all autotransitions as structurally zero and compute expected frequencies with IPF. At lags greater than 1 absolute compute expected frequencies using CK (equation (8.24)).
TEST	If the repeat code check option was *yes*, proceed as if NREP had been specified. If the repeat code check option was *no*, proceed as if MREP had been specified. TEST is the default.

by the numbers themselves. Such a convention may be acceptable for the data file. However, for labeling output, and for specifying pooling using the Pool command, as described in the next section, it is considerably more convenient if GSEQ has available labels or names instead.

The Variables, or Vars, command allows the user to assign names to variables and to their levels. Its general form is

VARIABLES *vname1* = 1 (*lname1* = 1 ...) ... ;

where *vname* and *lname* represent variable and level names for the corresponding numbers, respectively. For example,

VARS Group=1 (Clinic=1 Non_Clinic=2);

labels the two levels of the Group factor Clinic and Non_Clinic, whereas

VARS Partner=1 (Mother=1 Peer=2 Alone=3)
Age=2 (9_mo=1 12_mo=2 15_mo=3);

labels the two variables, Partner and Age. The three levels for Partner are Mother, Peer, and Alone, whereas the three levels for Age represent 9, 12, and 15 months.

If present, the Vars command follows the Rename command if one is used, otherwise it follows the File command directly. Rules for naming variables and levels of variables follow the usual rules for naming codes.

Not all variables need be named, and even if a variable is named its levels do not need to be named. However, in order to name levels of a variable, the variable must be named as well.

8.4 Pooling tallies over subjects and variables

Recall that an SDIS data file consists of *sessions* (code specifications separated with semicolons) and *subjects* (code specifications terminated with slashes, which may in fact represent an individual, a dyad, a family, an infant at a particular age, and so on), and that subjects may be assigned to different cells in the design, that is, to various levels or combinations of levels of design variables (see chapter 3). Recall also that by default GSEQ produces one contingency table per subject per lag per design cell for each Target command in the GSEQ command file (see chapters 5 and 6).

The Pool command allows users to change the default of one table per subject per lag per design cell. Its general form is

POOL [+|NO+ : *|NO* : *vnames*] ;

where the plus sign refers to sessions, the asterisk refers to subjects, and *vnames* may be any of the variable names specified with a previous Variables command. More than one of the options separated by colons may be used, but, as the brackets imply, at least one is required. Thus

POOL + NO*;

indicates pooling over sessions, but not over subjects; in other words, it explicitly states the default. If the Pool command is not used, or if specifications are omitted, these specifications are assumed.

The default may be overridden in a number of ways. For example,

POOL NO+;

or

POOL NO+ NO*;

indicates no pooling over sessions (if omitted, NO* is assumed), and so produces one table for each session in the data per design cell. If 18 subjects were observed for two sessions each (i.e., the SDIS data file consisted of 36 blocks of code specifications terminated either with a semicolon or a slash), 36 tables would result (assuming no lags).

Similarly,

POOL *;

or

POOL + *;

indicates pooling over subjects within groups (if omitted, + is assumed), and so produces one table for each group or cell defined by the design (if no design information is given, one group is assumed). For example, for the infant attention study if the Vars command specifying levels for the partner and age variables as given in the previous section is assumed, nine tables would be produced (again assuming no lags), one for each partner at each age (pooling together data for all subjects whose data ended with the same design specification).

Finally, for logical completeness (even though we suspect that this specification will not be used much) and only if each subject (within a group or cell) is observed for the same number of sessions,

POOL NO+ *;

indicates pooling over subjects but not over sessions. If 18 subjects were observed for two sessions each (and if all subjects belonged to the same group), two tables would result, one for each session (this and subsequent examples assume no lags). GSEQ displays the number of subjects pooled, so you can determine whether subjects were observed for the same number of sessions.

Users may also pool over levels of a variable or research factor. Thus

POOL Partner;

or

POOL + * Partner;

indicates pooling over all levels of the partner variable. Any variable name occurring alone on the Pool command implies pooling over subjects and sessions as well (i.e., assumes + *). Thus pooling over partner (i.e., observations with mothers, peers, and alone) would produce three tables, one for each of the three ages. Similarly,

POOL Age;

indicates pooling over all sessions, subjects, and age groups, thus producing three tables, one each for observations with each partner. Finally,

POOL Partner Age;

indicates pooling over all sessions, subjects, partners, and ages. The result would be a single contingency table.

In the event that the same number of subjects (presumably the same subjects) is observed at each level of a factor, the specifications allowed on the Pool command may be combined. Thus

POOL NO* Partner;

or

POOL ı NO* Partner;

indicates pooling each subject's data (the + or pooling over sessions is assumed) over all partners, but not pooling over subjects. If 18 infants had been observed, this command would result in 54 tables, one for each infant at each of three ages. Similarly,

POOL NO* Age;

indicates pooling each subject's data over all ages, producing one table for each infant with each partner; and

POOL NO* Partner Age;

indicates pooling each subject's data over all partners and ages, producing one table for each infant. When NO* and a variable name are specified, information displayed by GSEQ lets you determine whether the number of subjects is the same across levels of the variable.

In the event that the same number of sessions are observed for each subject, and still assuming that the same number of subjects is observed at each level of a factor,

POOL NO+ Partner;

or

POOL NO+ NO* Partner;

indicates pooling each session's data over partners, but not pooling over sessions or subjects (NO* is assumed). If 18 infants had been observed for two sessions each, 108 tables would result, one for each session per subject per age group. When NO+ is specified, information displayed by GSEQ lets you determine whether the numbers of sessions and subjects are the same across levels of a factor.

Finally, and again for logical completeness,

POOL NO+ * *vname*;

indicates pooling over subjects and levels of the variable named but not over sessions. It would be used only if the same number of subjects is observed at each level of the factor and each subject is observed the same number of sessions at each level; again, information displayed by GSEQ lets you determine whether this is the case.

If used at all, the Pool command (like the Stats, Title, and data modification commands), applies to the table or tables produced by the following Target command, and to all tables produced thereafter by subsequent Target commands, until another Pool command (if any) is encountered in the GSEQ command file (in which case the new Pool command resets previous Pool specifications).

8.5 Specifying simple frequencies, probabilities, and rates

GSEQ is primarily designed for sequential analysis. Thus the Stats command, which computes joint frequencies, transitional probabilities, adjusted residuals, chi-squares, and so forth for two-dimensional tables, is of central importance. However, simple or unconditional probabilities, displayed in one-dimensional tables, are often useful for basic descriptive purposes. Such simple statistics are requested with the Simple command, whose general form is

SIMPLE *stat_specs* { (*codes*) } ;

The statistical specifications recognized by GSEQ for the Simple command include FREQ, RELF, RATE, DURA, RELD, PROB, and AVGD; ALL can also be specified, in which case all simple statistics suitable for the data type are computed. Code names, enclosed in parentheses, may follow the statistical specifications, in which case the requested statistics are displayed just for the codes listed. Otherwise, the specified statistics are displayed for all codes currently declared (i.e., the original codes in the data file plus any new codes created with data modification commands).

The Simple command may be placed anywhere in the GSEQ command file that a Target command might appear, and as with the Target command, any previous data modification commands are taken into account. Simple statistics are then computed for each subject in the data file or, if a Pool command is used, are pooled before computation as indicated by that command. Permissible simple statistics are defined and described in the following paragraphs.

Unconditional frequencies, or *simple frequencies*, for all codes in the file (for each subject or other segment specified by the Pool command) are specified with FREQ, defined as the number of episodes or bouts for each code. For ESD, SSD, and TSD this is simply the number of times each code appears in the file, as you would expect. For ISD, it is the number of onsets, that is, the number of intervals containing the code preceded by an interval that does not, which is a consequence of our defining frequency as bout frequency. As discussed shortly, for ISD the number of intervals checked for each code is given with the DURA specification.

Relative frequencies for all codes in the file (for each subject or other segment specified by the Pool command) are specified with RELF. This is the number of episodes for each code divided by the number of episodes for all codes; hence the relative frequencies for a segment necessarily sum to 1. This statistic may not be meaningful for ISD, but is computed if requested.

Rates for all codes in the file (for each subject or other segment specified by the Pool command) are specified with RATE, which is defined as

$$rate = \frac{f(code)}{total\_time} factor \qquad (8.26)$$

where the total time is derived from the SDIS data file. The factor defaults to 60; thus, if the time unit is a second, rates per minute are given. But another factor can be specified, in which case it is signaled by an asterisk after RATE. Thus

SIMPLE RATE*3600;

indicates that the total number of tallies for a particular code is first divided by total time and then multiplied by 3,600. If time units were one second, then the rate would be expressed in occurrences per hour (60 seconds per minute, 60 minutes per hour, hence the 3,600 factor). The rate specification is ignored if the file is interval sequential (for which rate makes little sense) or if the file is event sequential and not all segments being pooled contain start and stop times (in which case total time in not known).

Durations for all codes in the file (for each subject or other segment specified by the Pool command) are specified with DURA. Duration is the total time coded for each code, which is straightforward for SSD and TSD files. It makes little sense for ESD; if requested, the specification is ignored. For ISD files, duration is defined as the total number of intervals checked, which may be more meaningful than the information given by FREQ for ISD files (number of bouts). In addition, when data are ISD, GSEQ computes estimates of duration according to Suen and Ary's (1989, p. 87) post-hoc corrections, which, in the case of partial and whole interval sampling (see chapter 4), tend to reduce bias due to the sampling technique. The correction for partial interval sampling is

Duration estimate = (DURA - FREQ) * interval width

and for whole interval sampling is

Duration estimate = (DURA + FREQ) * interval width

Table 8.3. *Simple command: Statistical specifications.*

Spec	Interpretation
FREQ	Simple or unconditional frequency (bouts)
RELF	Relative frequency
RATE	Rate (occurrences per time unit)
DURA	Duration
RELD	Relative duration
PROB	Simple or unconditional probability
AVGD	Mean bout duration
ALL	All of the above that apply

whereas for momentary sampling it is

$$\text{Duration estimate} = \text{DURA} * \text{interval width}$$

Although DURA is expressed in intervals, the estimates are expressed in time units, according to the interval width specified in the data file, and are printed next to the DURA column. No estimates are printed for momentary sampling with an interval width equal to 1 time unit.

Relative durations for all codes in the file (for each subject or other segment specified by the Pool command) are specified with RELD. This is the duration for each code divided by the sum of the durations for all codes; thus relative durations for a segment, like relative frequencies, necessarily sum to 1. For ESD, this specification is ignored. For other data types, relative durations make most sense when codes cannot co-occur and when codes are relatively exhaustive. Especially when codes co-occur, relative durations may not be readily interpretable, but are nonetheless computed if requested.

Unconditional probabilities, or *simple probabilities* (for all codes in the file for each subject or other segment specified by the Pool command), are specified with PROB. Probabilities for ESD codes are given by their relative frequencies, so PROB is ignored for ESD files. For other data types, durations are divided by total time or total number of intervals, as you would expect. Simple probabilities for a segment do not necessarily sum to 1. If codes co-occur, then their sum may be greater than 1; if they are not exhaustive, it may be less than 1.

Finally, the *average bout duration* (or mean episode length) for all codes in the file (for each subject or other segment specified by the Pool command) is specified with AVGD. This is the duration for each code divided by its frequency. Mean duration makes no sense for ESD, and if specified is ignored. This and other specifications for the Simple command are summarized in Table 8.3.

8.6 Saving frequencies for subsequent log-linear analyses

GSEQ computes useful descriptive (and inferential) statistics for two-dimensional tables. It also provides an export capability for those users who wish to pursue log-linear analyses of multidimensional frequency tables subsequently. The general form for the Export command is

EXPORT "filename" { SPSS I BMDP I ILOG} { OVERWRITE } ;

This command causes GSEQ to write a file that can be used as input to SPSS, BMDP, ILOG (Bakeman & Robinson, 1994), or other log-linear analysis programs. The SPSS and BMDP files will need further editing. If no parameter is given, the file contains one line for each cell in the tables selected. Index information for each cell appears first, followed by the frequency count for that cell. If SPSS or BMDP is specified, SPSS or BMDP commands precede the data saved. If ILOG is specified, or if no parameter is given, then the file can be read by the ILOG program. Filenames follow DOS conventions. If no extension is specified, SPS, INP, or DAT is used if SPSS, BMDP, or no parameter is specified, respectively. If ILOG is specified, extension IDF is used, overriding any extension given by the user.

8.7 Summary

In this chapter we showed how to specify a number of statistics, primarily ones based on the contingency tables GSEQ produces, but also some simple descriptive statistics as well. We also demonstrated how to provide names or labels for any design variables specified and for the levels of those variables, and how to pool observations in a number of different ways over sessions, subjects, and levels (see Tables 8.4 and 8.5). Except for some additional specifications concerned primarily with file selection, this completes our description of GSEQ, and its flexibility and capability. In the remaining chapters, we provide information about GSEQ of a more technical sort (e.g., how to run SDIS and GSEQ) and provide a few examples of specific analyses and problems.

Table 8.4. *GSEQ punctuation introduced in chapter 8.*

Mark	Interpretation
(	A left parenthesis begins lists of level names for the Variables command, an option for the Stats command, and lists of codes for the Simple command, and optionally precedes row indices in the Zeros command.
)	A right parenthesis ends lists of level names for the Variables command, an option for the Stats command, and lists of codes for the Simple command, and optionally follows column indices in the Zeros command.
=	On the Variables command, an equals sign separates variable and level names or labels from their corresponding numbers.
+	On the Pool command, a plus sign indicates pooling over sessions.
*	On the Pool command, an asterisk indicates pooling over subjects.
*	On the Simple command, an asterisk after the RATE specification and before a number indicates that the number is a multiplication factor for the rate computation.

Table 8.5. *GSEQ commands introduced in chapter 8.*

Command	Parameters
STATS	*stat_specs* { (*options*) } ;
ZEROS	(*row1* , *col1*) { (*row2* , *col2*) } ... ;
VARS	*vname1* = 1 (*lname1* = 1 ...) ... ;
POOL	[+|NO+ : *|NO* : *vnames*] ;
SIMPLE	*stat_specs* { (*codes*) } ;
EXPORT	"*filename*" { SPSS | BMDP | ILOG } { OVERWRITE } ;

Note: A vertical line separates choices when only one may be selected; a colon separates choices when more than one may be selected. Choices enclosed in braces are optional; choices enclosed in brackets are mandatory.

9

Running SDIS and GSEQ: The SDIS-GSEQ user interface

Topics covered in this chapter include:

1. How to use the Help command to learn about SGUI (the SDIS-GSEQ user interface).
2. How to use SGUI to select a current directory.
3. How to use SGUI to edit ASCII text files using an editor you supply.
4. How to use SGUI to run the SDIS and GSEQ programs.

The SDIS and GSEQ programs can be run from a DOS command prompt but are more easily invoked from SGUI, the SDIS-GSEQ user interface. In this relatively brief chapter, we explain how the user interface works. Additional help is available on-line.

9.1 SGUI basics

The SDIS-GSEQ package comprises six files, all of which must be in the same directory. The main file and the one you run to get started is SGUI.EXE. It then calls on SGUI.HLP (to display help text), SDIS.EXE (to check SDS files and convert them to MDS format), and GSEQ.EXE, GSEQA.EXE, and GSEQS.EXE (to perform GSEQ functions such as checking GSEQ specifications, modifying data, tallying results, and computing statistics).

Displayed at the top of the screen is the SGUI main menu:

GSEQ	SDIS	Edit	Projects	Applications	Dos	Info

The desired command can be selected in one of two ways. Use the left or right arrow keys to highlight your choice and then press **Enter** (or the down arrow), or simply press the key corresponding to the highlighted character (e.g., **S** for the SDIS). If you have a mouse, you can also move the cursor to the appropriate word and click. When selected, each of the main commands displays a pop-down list of subcommands, some of which have their own subcommands (as indicated by ->). Subcommands are selected in the same way as main commands

When you are done and want to exit the program, select **DOS** and then **eXit** or type **Alt+X** (hold down the Alt and X keys concurrently).

9.2 Getting help

The **F1** key (function key 1) provides context sensitive help. Thus, to learn how the interface works and what it can do, initially we recommend you browse among the various commands and subcommands, press **F1**, and read the text displayed. One feature is particularly helpful, both initially and later on. When you position the highlight to the SDIS main menu item and ask for help (i.e., press **F1**), a brief guide to SDIS syntax is provided. Similarly, when you position the highlight to the GSEQ main menu item and ask for help, a brief guide to GSEQ commands is provided. In the help windows, cross-references are displayed in a different color. To select one, just use the arrow keys to highlight your choice and press **Enter**.

9.3 Selecting directories

Directories provide a convenient way to organize your work, and you may want to create several different directories for different projects. When running SGUI, or most DOS programs for that matter, it is important to know which directory is current because files are read from and written to this directory. When first invoked, SGUI's current directory is the directory containing the six program files. You may change the current directory in two ways. First, you may enter a new directory name directly (select **DOS**, then **Change dir**), or you may select a project (**Projects**, **Select project**).

Before you select a project, you must define a list of project names and their corresponding directories (**Projects**, **Edit project list**). This is a convenient way to maintain a list of your active projects. Then all SDIS and GSEQ files related to particular projects, or aspects of your investigation, can be kept together in separate directories.

The name of the current directory and the project, if one is selected, are displayed at the bottom of the screen and written to a file

(SGUI.CFG) when you exit. They remain in effect for subsequent SGUI runs until you change them explicitly.

9.4 Editing files

In the process of doing their work, SDIS and GSEQ refer to a number of ASCII text files. These include SDIS files (files that contain data in SDIS format and have an extension of SDS), GSEQ files (files that contain GSEQ commands and have an extension of GSQ), and OUTPUT files (files that contain output from GSEQ and have an extension of OUT). Often you will want to edit these files; for example, when first checking SDS files for errors or later when specifying and checking various GSEQ commands. You could first leave the interface program and then invoke a word processor or an ASCII text editor. But then you would have to return to SGUI to run the corrected file. This is easy to do with a shell like *Windows*, but somewhat cumbersome with DOS itself or many DOS shells.

If you do not use Windows, you can still edit files without leaving SGUI. First name a text editor of your choice (**Edit, Add editor/Change editor**) and then enter the name of the executable file containing your editing program, including its path if it is not in the same directory as the interface programs. The name of any text editor selected is displayed at the bottom of the screen and, like the current directory, remains in effect until changed explicitly. Then later on when you select **Edit**, the editing program you specified is invoked. A fast-loading ASCII editor saves considerable time and, unless you use a shell like *Windows*, which allows you to swap among programs, we strongly recommend that you use one.

You also choose the file to edit using the **Edit** menu. It can be the current GSEQ or SDIS file (the names of which are displayed at the bottom of the screen), another file you name explicitly, or one you pick when browsing through files and directories on the disk. You may pick a file from a list of the most recently edited files: SGUI maintains a list of the last ten files that were edited during the current or preceding sessions, and these can be accessed by selecting **Pick recent files**. Or, if you select **Pick file**, all files in the current directory are displayed along with any lower-order directories, which are indicated with a slash following their name. Two dots followed by a slash indicates a higher-order directory. Selecting either the higher- or lower-order directory displays files and any lower-order directories associated with the new directory. Thus you can select any file on the current disk to edit. (One dot followed by a slash indicates the current directory; selecting it has no effect.)

Table 9.1. *Default settings for SDIS options.*

Option	Default
Echo	YES
Summary file	NO
Definition file	YES
MDS file	YES
Case sensitivity	YES
Exclusivity check	YES
Repeated code check	NO
Stop after 30 errors	YES
Ask confirmation	YES

9.5 Running SDIS and GSEQ

If you are just beginning to explore SDIS and GSEQ, you may begin by creating small test files using your ASCII editor. Or, you may already have SDIS files prepared. In any case, your first step is to select an SDIS file for processing. As with files you edit, you can name that file explicitly (**SDIS, Filename**) or browse for it (**SDIS, Pick file**). Once selected, you then run SDIS (**SDIS, Run SDIS**) and note any error or other messages displayed on the screen. You can also change SDIS options or reset those options to their default values. The help text (press **F1**) explains various options, but if you plan to run GSEQ later, the **Definition file** and **MDS file** options must be set to *yes*.

GSEQ works the same way. First you select a GSEQ command file to process, either explicitly or by browsing, and then you run the program, again noting any messages and output on the screen. GSEQ output is written to a file whose name is the same as the GSEQ command file, but whose extension is OUT. GSEQ output is displayed on the screen if the **Echo** option is set to *yes*. The amount of output can be reduced by setting the **Verbose** option to *no*. (Like the current directory, project, and SDIS and GSEQ files, option settings are preserved in the configuration file and once set remain in effect until changed explicitly.)

Both SDIS and GSEQ include a number of useful options (see Tables 9.1 and 9.2). These are not explained in detail here. Instead, we encourage you to read the help text associated with them. Simply select each option on your screen and press **F1**.

Table 9.2. *Default settings for GSEQ options.*

Option	Default
Echo	YES
Semicolons	YES
Verbose	YES
Pagination	YES
Overwrite output	NO
Output width	80 cols
ASCII print	NORMAL
Ask confirmation	YES

9.6 Summary

In this chapter we have described how to run the SDIS and GSEQ programs using SGUI, the SDIS-GSEQ user interface. We have shown how to use the Help command to learn what the interface can do, how to select a current directory, how to edit the various ASCII text files SDIS and GSEQ use (using an editor of your choice), and how to run the SDIS and GSEQ programs themselves. In the next and final chapter we give examples of how SDIS and GSEQ can be used to represent and analyze sequential data from a few typical yet relatively complicated research endeavors.

10

Advanced GSEQ: Practical problems and solutions

SDIS and GSEQ are powerful and flexible tools, and often they can be used to solve problems in ways that may not be obvious at first glance. A number of interesting solutions are presented in this chapter. Particular topics covered in this chapter include:

1. How to determine whether observers can detect particular kinds of episodes reliably and, once detected, whether they then code the episodes reliably.
2. How to perform event-based analyses (e.g., describing sequences and co-occurrences of episodes) even when data are recorded initially in a time-based format (i.e., SSD or TSD).
3. How to take the identity of particular participants and the inter-active context itself into account when analyzing sequences of events.

Throughout this book we have clung to our categorization of four data types (event, state, timed event, and interval sequential data). Indeed, SDIS requires that you declare data type at the outset, and the data type sometimes limits features and statistics you can request. In chapter 2 we introduced four studies, each representing a different data type, and then proceeded to use codes from those four paradigmatic studies as examples throughout subsequent chapters.

Nonetheless, we recognize two qualifications. First, the boundaries between the data types are occasionally fuzzy. Sometimes the same data may be expressed as more than one type (although ultimately, all data types are represented with a common format in the MDS files that GSEQ processes). Second, not all studies produce data that fall neatly into one of these four types. Sometimes no type may appear to fit, other times different aspects of the same data may seem better suited to one or another of the four types. In this final chapter, we introduce a fifth para-digmatic study and use it to demonstrate how different SDIS data types and GSEQ features might be used in its analysis. The larger purpose is to demonstrate some of the surprisingly flexible uses for SDIS and GSEQ features – uses that may not be readily apparent from a casual reading of the preceding chapters.

10.1 Analyzing episodes: The child negotiation study

What we call the child negotiation study here is a greatly simplified version of one conceived by David Bearison with the help of Bruce Dorval and other colleagues at the Graduate School and University Center of the City University of New York. It reflects the complexity many researchers seek to capture. Like many of their colleagues, these researchers use videorecorders initially to preserve behavior of interest. Subsequently, coders view the videotapes, and then detect and record occurrences of various behaviors. Often onset times for some behaviors, and onset and offset times for others, are noted, using the time display that is easily made a part of the picture with the video equipment readily available today.

Bearison is not interested in every moment on the tape, only in certain times when the children (who have been instructed to co-invent a board game) enter into what he terms a *negotiation episode*. Asking coders first to identify episodes of a certain kind before moving on to other coding tasks is a relatively common and useful strategy. For example, other investigators might be interested in episodes of children's conflict or cooperation, spouses' argument or tenderness, and client-therapist stalemate or breakthrough.

Agreement in detecting episodes

In all such cases, coders first identify the episodes of interest, usually by identifying their onset and offset times. The first task is to establish observer agreement by determining, for example, whether two observers independently identify the same episodes. In effect, observers are asked to segment the stream of behavior into two states, episode occurring or no episode occurring. Because we are comparing two observers' coding, different codes are used to identify each observer. For example, we might use A1 and A2 to identify episodes detected by the first and second observer, respectively.

Either a TSD or a SSD file would work. Thus the same 10 seconds could be coded either as

> Timed A1 A2;
> ,1   A1,1-3) A1,7-8) &
> A2,1-4) A2,8 ,10)/

or

```
State (A1 N1) (A2 N2);
A1=3 N1=3 A1=2 N1=2 &
A2=4 N2=3 A2=1 N2=2 /
```

(where N1 and N2 indicate no episode as coded by the first and second observer, respectively). Then kappa could be computed using either

```
FILE "TSD_file_name";
TITLE "Compute Kappa";
STATS KAPPA;
TARGET A1 &;
GIVEN A2 &;
```

or

```
FILE "SSD_file_name";
TITLE "Compute Kappa";
STATS KAPPA;
TARGET A1 N1;
GIVEN A2 N2;
```

as input to GSEQ (you may want to verify both by hand calculation and GSEQ that the value of kappa for these sample data is 0.6).

Agreement in coding episodes

Once identified, a number of coding schemes might be applied to episodes. For example, Bearison defines two sets of mutually exclusive and exhaustive codes, one for the topic and another for the outcome of negotiation episodes. For the moment, let us consider only the first such scheme applied. Imagine that three codes are defined (e.g., A, B, and C). In principle, this is not much different from the scheme suggested earlier for episodes (A and N), except that now the stream of behavior is segmented into four states instead of two (A, B, C, and N), where the N or no-episode code insures that the set is exhaustive.

Often one coder is designated the data coder and the other the reliability checker. It makes sense to use codes such as A, B, C, and N for the data coder and codes such as A2, B2, C2, and N2 for the reliability checker. The exact form is unimportant, as long as codes for the same behavior coded by different observers can be distinguished. As noted earlier, assuming that onset and offset times are recorded, either TSD or SSD could be used to represent such data. The SDIS files compiled by the data coder would then be used for subsequent analyses. Other SDIS files, formed by combining codes from the two observers for those portions of the corpus coded by both, could then be used for additional reliability checks.

When observers are asked to detect episodes, no matter how those episodes are themselves coded further, the reliability with which the observers detect the episodes in the first place needs to be established. The time-based procedure demonstrated in the previous section seems the best way to do this (tallying whether or not each time unit is coded as occurring during an episode) because observers, in effect, get credit for agreeing both when an episode did and did not occur.

When the episodes are themselves coded, reliability checking can be accomplished in essentially the same way. Assume that each episode is coded with respect to three schemes, each represented with a set of ME&E codes (as noted earlier, the first scheme might include codes for the topic of the episode, the second scheme codes for its outcome, and so forth). The reliability for each scheme would then be established with a time-based kappa, exactly as described earlier for the episode-detecting kappa. Again, separate SDIS files would be prepared, one for each scheme, but this time the number of codes per observer would be greater than two.

Alternatively, episode-based kappas could be computed, in which case each episode detected by both observers would add one tally to a kappa table. Again, separate files would be prepared for each scheme, combining codes from both observers, but this time using ISD instead of SSD or TSD. For example,

> Interval (A B C) (A2 B2 C2);
> A A2, B B2, B A2, C C2 /

represents four episodes. Here the data are regarded as interval sequential, and each episode detected by both observers is treated as though it occupied an interval. As you can see, for this example the observers agreed on the first, second, and fourth episodes and disagreed about the third. As for the time-based kappa, the episode-based kappa would have one kappa table (and one SDIS file) for each scheme.

Almost always, we prefer the time-based approach because we think it more faithfully reflects the moment-by-moment decision making we expect of observers when detecting and coding episodes in an ongoing stream of behavior. Moreover, it gives them credit for knowing both when to code and when not to code an episode. The event-based approach, on the other hand, with its far fewer tallies, considers only episodes detected by both observers.

Descriptive statistics for episodes

Imagine that we have created a tiny SDIS file that looks like

> State (A B C N);
> A=3 N=3 B=2 N=1 A=1 /

or

> State (A B C N);
> ,1 A,1 N,4 B,7 N,9 A,10 ,11 /

or

> Timed (A B C);
> ,1 A,1-3) B,7-8) A,10) /

What then? Almost certainly we would want simple descriptive statistics. The following GSEQ commands:

> FILE "*TSD_file_name*";
> TITLE "Compute Descriptive Statistics";
> SIMPLE ALL;

would produce the following output:

Codes	FREQ	RELF	RATE	DURA	RELD	PROB	AVGD
A	2	0.6667	12.0000	4	0.6667	0.4000	2.00
B	1	0.3333	6.0000	2	0.3333	0.2000	2.00
C	0	0.0000	0.0000	0	0.0000	0.0000	0.00
Totals:	3	1.0000	18.0000	6	1.0000	0.6000	

Total number of time units: 10

whereas

> FILE "*SSD_file_name*";
> TITLE "Compute Descriptive Statistics";
> SIMPLE ALL;

would produce:

Codes	FREQ	RELF	RATE	DURA	RELD	PROB	AVGD
A	2	0.4000	12.0000	4	0.4000	0.4000	2.00
B	1	0.2000	6.0000	2	0.2000	0.2000	2.00
C	0	0.0000	0.0000	0	0.0000	0.0000	0.00
N	2	0.4000	12.0000	4	0.4000	0.4000	2.00
Totals:	5	1.0000	30.0000	10	1.0000	1.0000	

Total number of time units: 10

The example SSD and TSD files used here appear almost identical. For both, A was coded twice and B once during the 10-second session, and for both, A and B lasted the same amount of time. Thus for both, the frequencies, rates, durations, probabilities, and average durations are the same.

The relative frequencies and durations are somewhat different, however. Recall that simple statistics for specific codes can be requested (codes are enclosed in parentheses). Then for the SSD file given earlier,

SIMPLE ALL (A B C N);

and

SIMPLE ALL;

produce identical output. When no codes are listed on the Simple command, all codes declared in the SDIS file, or created using data modification commands, are used. In this case, the state sequential file includes the no episode or N code, whereas the timed event sequential file does not.

When GSEQ computes relative frequencies and durations, only the codes listed are taken into account. Thus a code's relative frequency is the number of times this code appeared in the file relative to the number of times all codes listed on the Simple command (explicitly or implicitly) appeared. Likewise, a code's relative duration is the number of units this code lasted relative to the *total* number of units all codes lasted. For example, if the SDIS file were

Timed A B C;
,1 A,1-6) B,3-8) ,10) /

and the Simple command requested all statistics (for all codes), GSEQ would produce:

Codes	FREQ	RELF	RATE	DURA	RELD	PROB	AVGD
A	1	0.5000	6.0000	6	0.5000	0.6000	6.00
B	1	0.5000	6.0000	6	0.5000	0.6000	6.00
C	0	0.0000	0.0000	0	0.0000	0.0000	0.00
Totals:	2	1.0000	12.0000	12	1.0000	1.2000	

Total number of time units: 10

As can be seen, for timed event sequential data, relative durations for the individual codes, and the total for the probabilities may not make much sense. The relative durations will always sum to 1 by definition, but the base may include more or less time than in the actual session (as indicated by the total of the durations, here 12); it depends on the codes listed and whether they overlap in time. Similarly, the sum of the probabilities may be more or less than 1, again depending on the circumstances just stated. Otherwise, the statistics displayed for codes in TSD files, when all simple ones are requested, are easily interpretable. In particular, the probabilities are the proportion of time units assigned to the listed code relative to the total number of time units in the session, as you would expect.

One final note: Remembering the ampersand as used on the Target and Given commands, and wanting to create a new, null code for a TSD file (like the N code in the SSD file earlier), you might be tempted to specify

SIMPLE ALL (A B C &);

but this would produce an error message because the Simple command computes statistics only for codes declared in the SDIS file or created by means of data modification commands.

Describing sequences of episodes

It might be useful to know whether sequences of episodes were patterned as occurs, for example, when one negotiation topic follows another at greater than chance rates. If this were our only question, then we would have produced a simple ESD data file in the first place. But we have already prepared a SSD or TSD file containing not just the sequence of topics (more generally, a sequence of codes where each belongs to a single ME&E set), but time information for the episodes as well (because we wanted the sorts of simple statistics described in the previous section). Can we make use of the existing file, thereby saving ourselves the trouble of creating an ESD file?

The answer is yes. Assuming that the SSD or TSD file contains a single stream of (ME&E) coded episodes, then the GSEQ commands

```
FILE "SSD_file_name";
TITLE "Create and tally lag 1 event statistics";
EVENT;
REMOVE N;
TARGET *; LAG 1;
```

or

```
FILE "TSD_file_name";
TITLE "Create and tally lag 1 event statistics";
EVENT;
TARGET *; LAG 1;
```

would first create an ESD version of the file and then compute lag 1 tallies. The SSD file contains an explicit not-in-episode code (N), which is removed from consideration (because we want to analyze a sequence like A B A, not A N B N A). Otherwise the procedure is the same for SSD and TSD files. Given the TSD file described earlier, which was

>   Timed (A B C);
>   ,1 A,1-3) B,7-8) A,10) /

or the SSD version of the same stream, the GSEQ commands just given would produce the following table:

```
Tallies are events.
Lag 1
JNTF.  Observed lag frequencies:

Given      Target
             A        B        C      Totals

A            0        1        0        1
B            1        0        0        1
C            0        0        0        0

Totals       1        1        0        2
```

In this tiny example there were two lag 1 transitions, one from episodes coded A to B and another from B to A.

Describing co-occurrences of episodes

When episodes are coded on more than one dimension (i.e., more than one set of ME&E codes is used, such as one for topic and another for the outcome of negotiation episodes), you may want to describe co-occurrences, asking, for example, how often a particular topic was associated with a particular outcome. Assume that topic (the first dimension) is coded A, B, or C and that outcome (the second dimension) is coded X, Y, or Z. To describe co-occurrences, codes from both sets need to appear in the same file. For example, a TSD file combining both topic and outcome might look like this:

>   Timed (A B C) (X Y Z);
>   ,1 A,1-3) B,7-8) A,10) &
>   X,1-3) X,7-8) Z,10) /

If our only interest were in co-occurrences, we might have created an ISD file in the first place, letting each interval represent an episode. Such a file might look like this:

Interval ($topic = A B C) ($outcome = X Y Z);
A X, B X, A Z/

Then

FILE "*ISD_file_name*";
TITLE "Tally topic and outcome co-occurrences";
TARGET $outcome; GIVEN $topic;

would produce the desired joint frequency counts. From it we would learn that X and A, B and X, and A and Z all co-occurred once.

Still, if we have already prepared a TSD (or SSD) file, why not make use of it? There is no reason to prepare a separate ISD file. If we were to specify

FILE "*TSD_file_name*";
TITLE "Tally topic, outcome time co-occurrences";
TARGET X Y Z &; GIVEN A B C &;

GSEQ would give us the following, time-based result:

Given	Target				
	X	Y	Z	&	Totals
A	3	0	1	0	4
B	2	0	0	0	2
C	0	0	0	0	0
&	0	0	0	4	4
Totals	5	0	1	4	10

indicating that X and A co-occurred for 3 time units, B and X for 2, and A and Z for just 1 time unit. But this may not be what we want. If we want co-occurrences, not for time units but for the episodes themselves, then we would specify

FILE "*TSD_file_name*";
TITLE "Tally topic, outcome episode co-occurrences";
WINDOW XE = (X;
WINDOW YE = (Y;
WINDOW ZE = (Z;
WINDOW AE = (A;
WINDOW BE = (B;
WINDOW CE = (C;
TARGET XE YE ZE; GIVEN AE BE CE;

In this case, GSEQ would produce the following, episode-based result (even though tallying from the TSD file):

Given	Target			
	XE	YE	ZE	Totals
AE	1	0	1	2
BE	1	0	0	1
CE	0	0	0	0
Totals	2	0	1	3

Here the Window command is used to define new codes, each of which represents the onset of a topic or outcome episode. By definition, there can only be one onset per episode, so if only onsets are listed on the Target and Given commands, the number of tallies entered in the table will necessarily be the number of episodes. If the timing for the two streams is the same, as here, then the numbers of onset and episode co-occurrences are necessarily the same.

10.2 Analyzing events in context

Like many investigators, Bearison and his colleagues are interested in more than the occurrence, classification, and sequencing of the episodes themselves. They also want to probe what goes on within episodes. To that end, they do what many other investigators of streams of talk or conversation do: They segment the stream into speaking turns (or *thought units*, where a turn might contain one or more thought units), and then code each such turn or unit. The length of these turns is not of much interest, so their onset times are not recorded. But the speaker, the function of his or her turn, and other aspects related to it are very much of interest.

Coding schemes that characterize conversation (e.g., between peers, parents and children, or therapists and clients) fill the literature. At a formal level, their overall structure is the same as that introduced earlier for episodes: Both thought-unit-like and episode-like schemes can be described as consisting of sets of ME&E codes. Many investigators work solely with thought-unit-like schemes, but others, such as Bearison, introduce another level of complexity: They nest conversational-turn coding within encompassing episodes, which are also coded. In fact, the episodes serve as a context for the coded conversation.

Aggregating and disaggregating speaker and other codes

Whether or not coded conversation is nested within episodes, the issue of speaker often arises. Indeed, many coding schemes have a grammar-like structure, consisting of a speaker, an action, and often the object, the indirect object, and so forth (e.g., Juan gives Maria the book). As a general rule, for SDIS and GSEQ purposes we think such schemes are best represented, initially at least, with single codes, as exemplified by the marital talk study introduced in chapter 2. For example, codes for a marital interaction study might have the general form *saaaeee*, where *s* signifies speaker (e.g., H for husband or W for wife), *aaa* the action (e.g., Com, Emp, and so forth), and *eee* an emotional valence (e.g., Pos or Neg). Then, for some purposes, the antecedents and consequences of, for example, HComPos and HComNeg could be tallied separately. But for other purposes, a new code could be used. For example,

> RECODE HCom = HComPos HComNeg;

would combine all husband complaints no matter their valence.

Usually when time duration is not an issue, SDIS data are expressed as event sequences. Here is a simple example:

> Event; . . . WEmpPos HNgtNeg WComNeg
> HAppNeg WComPos HComNeg WEmoPos HEmoNeg . . .

But these same data could be expressed as interval sequences instead. Then they might look like this:

> Interval =1; . . . W Emp Pos, H Ngt Neg, W Com Neg,
> H App Neg, W Com Pos, H Com Neg, W Emo Pos,
>   H Emo Neg, . . .

Here the ISD version disaggregates the separate aspects of the conversational turn. Thus H and W; Com, Emp, and so forth; and Pos and Neg all become separate codes. Again, as in an earlier example, the interval represents an event, not a particular time duration. This representation, compared to the event representation just given, may facilitate sequential tallying of each separate aspect (e.g., speaker, action, emotional valence).

In any event, the compound codes used for the ESD version can easily be aggregated from the ISD representation using the And command, by using, for example, the commands

> AND WEmpPos = W Emp Pos;
> AND HNgtNeg = H Ngt Neg;
> AND WComNeg = W Com Neg;
> AND WCom = W Com;
> AND HEmo = H Emo;

Commands like these show how any compound code of interest could be created. But which data type should be used, ESD or ISD? Partly it is a matter of taste. After all, with ESD, separate aspects can be disaggregated with the Recode command, whereas with ISD, compound aspects can be aggregated with the And command. Thus the tallies and statistics usually desired can be derived with essentially equal ease from both event and interval sequences.

Investigators whose data consist solely of coded conversation will probably prefer an event representation for its somewhat greater simplicity. But investigators like Bearison will probably prefer an interval representation for their turns of talk because this allows them to pose questions relatively easily, not just concerning the sequencing of events, but also concerning the context within which such sequencing takes place.

Context and interval sequences

Assume, for example, that Bearison codes speaker and function for each conversational turn (actually, he codes other aspects as well and uses more codes than we use here), and that speaker is represented with two codes (1 and 2) and function with codes such as Agre, Dis, Elab, Asrt, and Oth (for agreement, disagreement, elaboration, assertion, and other, respectively). Then the coding for the first three episodes detected might look like this:

```
Interval =1 (A B C) (X Y Z) (Agre Asrt Dis Elab Oth) (1 2);
A+ X+ 1 Asrt, 2 Dis, 1 Elab, 2 Oth, 2 Agre;
B+ X+ 2 Asrt, 1 Elab, 2 Dis, 1 Dis, 2 Agre;
A+ Z+ 1 Oth, 2 Agre, 1 Elab, 2 Oth, 1 Dis /
```

Here the episodes, which were represented earlier and for other purposes (i.e., to describe co-occurrences) as TSD, become context codes in an interval sequential data file, and each episode becomes a session (as identified by its terminating semicolon). As in the earlier example, the topic of the episode is coded A, B, or C, and the outcome X, Y, or Z.

Data such as these could be used to answer several questions, including: How are the function codes sequenced? How often are the function codes used by each speaker? Are some function codes associated more than others with specific topic codes? And are some function codes associated more than others with specific outcome codes? As an example, consider the following GSEQ commands:

```
FILE "ISD_file_name";
TITLE "Analyzing events in context.";
TARGET Agre Dis Elab Asrt Oth; LAG 1;
TARGET Agre Dis Elab Asrt Oth; GIVEN 1 2;
STATS CONP;
TARGET Agre Dis Elab Asrt Oth; GIVEN A B C;
TARGET Agre Dis Elab Asrt Oth; GIVEN X Y Z;
```

Output from the first Target command would look like this:

```
Tallies are intervals.
Lag 1
JNTF.  Observed lag frequencies:

Given     Target
               Agre    Dis    Elab    Asrt    Oth    Totals

Agre            0       0       1       0       0        1
Dis             1       1       1       0       0        3
Elab            0       1       0       0       2        3
Asrt            0       1       1       0       0        2
Oth             2       1       0       0       0        3

Totals          3       4       3       0       2       12
```

The first Target command was not paired with a Given command, so columns and rows have the same labels. This table gives the lag 1 transitions for the conversational turns occurring within the three negotiation episodes. You should verify that these tallies are correct.

Output from the second Target command would look like this:

```
Tallies are intervals.
Lag 0
JNTF.  Observed lag frequencies:

Given     Target
               Agre    Dis    Elab    Asrt    Oth    Totals

1               0       2       3       1       1        7
2               3       2       0       1       2        8

Totals          3       4       3       2       3       15
```

The number of times speaker 1 used each code appears on the first row; the second row displays similar counts for speaker 2.

Output from the third and fourth Target commands would look like this:

```
Tallies are intervals.
Lag 0

JNTF.  Observed lag frequencies:
Given     Target
               Agre    Dis    Elab    Asrt    Oth    Totals

A               2       2       2       1       3       10
B               1       2       1       1       0        5
C               0       0       0       0       0        0

Totals          3       4       3       2       3       15
```

```
CONP.   Conditional probabilities:
Given       Target
            Agre    Dis     Elab    Asrt    Oth

A         0.2000  0.2000  0.2000  0.1000  0.3000
B         0.2000  0.4000  0.2000  0.2000  0.0000
C         0.0000  0.0000  0.0000  0.0000  0.0000
```

```
JNTF.   Observed lag frequencies:
Given       Target
            Agre    Dis     Elab    Asrt    Oth     Totals

X             2       3       2       2       1       10
Y             0       0       0       0       0        0
Z             1       1       1       0       2        5

Totals        3       4       3       2       3       15
```

```
CONP.   Conditional probabilities:
Given       Target
            Agre    Dis     Elab    Asrt    Oth

X         0.2000  0.3000  0.2000  0.2000  0.1000
Y         0.0000  0.0000  0.0000  0.0000  0.0000
Z         0.2000  0.2000  0.2000  0.0000  0.4000
```

From these tables, we learn how often the conversation content codes (i.e., Agre, Dis, etc.) occurred within the context of different topics and outcomes. For example, we learn that disagreement was twice as likely during episodes of topic B than A (p[Dis|A] = .2; p[Dis|B] = .4), and half again as likely when X rather than Z was the outcome (p[Dis|X] = .3; p[Dis|Z] = .2).

The tables demonstrated here hardly exhaust all the possibilities, but they should serve to suggest the usefulness of expressing event sequences as sequences of coded intervals. Lagged sequential relations can be probed, exactly as with ESD, and differences in frequencies for the conversational content codes for different speakers easily computed. Moreover, the episodes within which the sequences are nested can be represented as context codes, and differences in frequencies for the conversational content codes within different contexts can be determined.

Even the co-occurrences of episodes can be determined, exactly as demonstrated previously for TSD files. For example, the GSEQ command file

> FILE "*ISD_file_name*";
> TITLE "Tally topic, outcome episode co-occurrences";
> WINDOW XE = (X;
> WINDOW YE = (Y;
> WINDOW ZE = (Z;

WINDOW AE = (A;
WINDOW BE = (B;
WINDOW CE = (C;
TARGET XE YE ZE; GIVEN AE BE CE;

would give exactly the same table displayed at the end of section 10.1 in the context of a TSD example. Specifically:

Given	Target XE	YE	ZE	Totals
AE	1	0	1	2
BE	1	0	0	1
CE	0	0	0	0
Totals	2	0	1	3

Yet another question of interest concerns whether certain transitions occur more frequently in some contexts than others. For example, imagine we want to determine whether the transition from assert to disagree is more likely during some topics than others. This could be accomplished in two ways. First, consider the following GSEQ file:

FILE "*ISD_file_name*";
TITLE "Analyzing sequences in context.";
AND AAsrt = A Asrt;
AND BAsrt = B Asrt;
AND CAsrt = C Asrt;
AND ADis = A Dis;
AND BDis = B Dis;
AND CDis = C Dis;
TARGET ADis A BDis B CDis C; LAG 1;
GIVEN AAsrt BAsrt CAsrt;

which produces the following output:

```
Tallies are intervals.
Lag 1
```

JNTF. Observed lag frequencies:

Given	Target ADis	A	BDis	B	CDis	C	Totals
AAsrt	1	0	0	0	0	0	1
BAsrt	0	0	0	1	0	0	1
CAsrt	0	0	0	0	0	0	0
Totals	1	0	0	1	0	0	2

The single lag 1 assert to disagree transition in our example data occurred during topic A, and is reflected by the value of 1 for $x_{1,1}$ or $x_{AAsrt,ADis}$ (the cell in the upper left). Another assert during topic B was not followed by disagree, and so the value of $x_{2,3}$ or $x_{BAsrt,BDis}$ is 0. With realistic data, we would expect many more tallies, although all would be in columns 1 and 2 of row 1, columns 3 and 4 of row 2, and columns 5 and 6 of row 3. Other cells, representing transitions from Asrt within one topic (i.e., episode) to some code within another topic are not logically possible.

Now an interesting and useful application of the hierarchical processing rule for target and given lists discussed in chapter 5 emerges. Intervals are scanned first for occurrences of the new code AAsrt, then BAsrt, and finally CAsrt (the given codes). None of these codes can co-occur in an interval, so no conflict is possible. Assume that an interval during topic B contains an Asrt code. Then the new code BAsrt would be found, and, depending on the contents of the next interval, a tally would be added to either column 3 or 4 of row 2.

The next interval is then scanned for the six target codes, left to right; if a match is found, a tally is added to the table, and scanning ceases. The first two target codes (ADis and A) cannot occur. The interval must contain a B code (the topic for this episode is B or else the previous interval would not contain a BAsrt), but it is examined first for the new code, BDis because BDis occurs before B on the target list. If the interval contains BDis (a BAsrt-BDis transition), then a tally is added to the third column, but if not, then a tally is added to the fourth column. And indeed, for our example tally, the value of $x_{2,4}$ or $x_{BAsrt,B}$ is 1, indicating a transition from Asrt to something other than Dis during an episode whose topic is B.

Thus the table contains not only counts for the three transitions of interest, but also totals for the number of asserts coded within each topic (in this case, one each for topics A and B, shown in the rightmost column). As a result, the conditional probabilities corresponding to the three critical cells, $x_{1,1}$ and $x_{2,3}$ and $x_{3,5}$, or $x_{AAsrt,ADis}$ and $x_{BAsrt,BDis}$ and $x_{CAsrt,CDis}$, are exactly the values we require: the $p(Dis_1|Asrt_0)$ within episodes of topics A, B, and C.

Context and event sequences

There is a second way to determine whether certain transitions occur more frequently in some contexts than others. Instead of using context codes, as just demonstrated, we could regard context as part of the design. For example, we could regard topic as the first design factor and outcome as the second. Thus the codes A, B, and C and X, Y, and Z become levels 1, 2, and 3 for these two factors. Then the ISD data shown earlier become

> Interval =1;
> 1 Asrt, 2 Dis, 1 Elab, 2 Oth, 2 Agre (1,1)/ % A, X %
> 2 Asrt, 1 Elab, 2 Dis, 1 Dis, 2 Agre (2,1)/ % B, X %
> 1 Oth, 2 Agre, 1 Elab, 2 Oth, 1 Dis (1,3)/ % A, Z %

Realistic data would include many episodes per cell and episodes for all possible cells; as with any data type, cells could contain data from one or more than one subject. Here only one episode per design cell and only three such cells (out of a possible nine) are shown. For these data, the following GSEQ commands:

> FILE "*ISD_file_name*";
> TARGET Dis &; LAG 1; GIVEN Asrt &;

would produce the following output:

```
Variable 1, condition 1.
Variable 2, condition 1.
Subject #1.  Subject number in current cell is 1.
Pooling over 1 session (maximum 1 session per subject).

Tallies are intervals.
Lag 1
JNTF.  Observed lag frequencies:

Given     Target
               Dis        &      Totals
        _____
Asrt            1          0        1
&               0          3        3
        _____
Totals  |       1          3   |    4
```

```
Variable 1, condition 1.
Variable 2, condition 3.
Subject #1.  Subject number in current cell is 1.
Pooling over 1 session (maximum 1 session per subject).

Tallies are intervals.
Lag 1
JNTF.  Observed lag frequencies:

Given     Target
               Dis        &      Totals
        _____
Asrt            0          0        0
&               1          3        4
        _____
Totals  |       1          3   |    4
```

```
Variable 1, condition 2.
Variable 2, condition 1.
Subject #1.  Subject number in current cell is 1.
Pooling over 1 session (maximum 1 session per subject).
```

```
Tallies are intervals.
Lag 1
JNTF.  Observed lag frequencies:

Given      Target
              Dis        &      Totals

Asrt          0          1        1
&             2          1        3

Totals        2          2        4
```

In this case, separate tables are presented for each design cell, whereas when context codes expressed topic and outcome information, as in the previous example, only one table resulted. But, as before, we observe one assert to disagree sequence for topic A and outcome X (cell$_{1,1}$ of the design); one assert code followed by something other than disagree for topic B and outcome X (cell$_{2,1}$ of the design); and no assert codes at all for topic A and outcome Z (cell$_{1,3}$ of the design). Given more realistic data, we would probably request various statistics (like conditional probabilities and adjusted residuals), might well expand the target and given lists, and could pool over levels of topic and outcome (see the Pool command as described in chapter 8) if collapsed statistics were desired.

In the previous example, ISD was used to capture the nesting of turns within episodes. Episodes were treated as sessions. Events within episodes were expressed as sequential intervals and context as explicit context codes assigned to all the intervals included in a given episode. In the current example, ISD was again used, but this time context was expressed as though it were part of the design. Episodes were still treated as sessions (and could be associated with different subjects), but now they were assigned to cells generated by the design (e.g., cell$_{1,1}$ for topic A and outcome X episodes).

The notation assigning sessions to cells of a design is not unique to ISD, however. If desired, the same way of expressing context could be used with any of the other data types. Consider our running example. Expressed as ESD, the data would look like this:

Event;
1Asrt 2Dis 1Elab 2Oth 2Agre (1,1)/ % A, X %
2Asrt 1Elab 2Dis 1Dis 2Agre (2,1)/ % B, X %
1Oth 2Agre 1Elab 2Oth 1Dis (1,3)/ % A, Z %

Then the GSEQ commands

FILE "*ESD_file_name*";
RECODE Asrt = 1Asrt 2Asrt;
RECODE Dis = 1Dis 2Dis;
TARGET Dis &; LAG 1; GIVEN Asrt &;

would produce exactly the same output just shown for the ISD version of these data.

Again the question arises, if context is expressed as design information, which data type is preferred, event or interval? We are not certain whether one or the other is always the clear winner. Instead, we suspect that individual inclination and circumstances will settle the matter. Some investigators may prefer the initial disaggregation made possible by interval representation, so will always use ISD no matter whether context is expressed explicitly with context codes before episodes or as design information after them. Others may prefer the initial aggregation compatible with ESD and may see no advantage to explicit context codes, and thus will opt for ESD.

10.3 Summary

As with coding, so with data representation. Some investigators favor splitting codes, and others lumping them. Both styles are easily accommodated with SDIS and GSEQ. This is perhaps one of the more important points to be gleaned from the examples presented in this chapter: SDIS and GSEQ are remarkably flexible. Often there is more than one way to represent data and more than one route to a desired statistic.

There is a second, perhaps even more important point that readers of this chapter should absorb: complex data often require different representations and many files. Often those of us imbued with the academic spirit seek single, all-encompassing answers. Perhaps as a corollary, we pursue data analysis in a similar vein, attempting to include all our data in one encompassing file, which is then subjected to one monster analysis from which, it is hoped, all answers will flow. Such an approach seldom works.

Instead, for most complex projects, different pieces of the data corpus resulting from initial coding will be represented in different ways, quite likely using different data types. Perhaps the best guiding principle is the one we freely give to others (and often forget for ourselves): For each coding scheme and for the coding distinctions made within each scheme, we should ask, What research question does this code (or distinction) answer? And exactly how will the resulting data be analyzed to provide answers to those questions?

But once the truly hard work of delineating questions, codes, and the required data files and analyses is done, the tools presented in this book can come into play. Good ideas are essential. A programmer who can reformat existing data files into SDIS format may be required. But beyond that, once the SDIS and GSEQ programs presented here are mastered, your ability to use sequential analysis productively should no longer be stymied by the technicalities of tallying and computing.

A

Installing and running SDIS and GSEQ

A.1 Diskette contents and installation

The diskette that comes with this book contains the following files:

INSTALL.EXE	Main install program
INSTALAR.BAT	
INST1.EXE	Installation programs
INST2.EXE	
SG1.EXE	Compressed SDIS-GSEQ programs
SG2.EXE	
EX1.EXE	Compressed example files
EX2.EXE	

The install program must be run from the diskette. Do not copy the files to your hard disk and then attempt to run the install program; it will not work. Instead, insert the diskette into drive A, type:

A:

and press **Enter** to change the default drive to A. Next type:

INSTALL

press **Enter** again, and follow the instructions. (If you wish, you may use B or any other floppy drive instead of A.)

The install program begins by asking which language you prefer, English or Spanish. Both English and Spanish versions of the SDIS-GSEQ programs are included, and both work exactly the same, except that if you use the Spanish version you must use Spanish names for the GSEQ commands (for example, ARCHIVO instead of FILE) and messages are in Spanish.

By default, the programs are installed in a directory called C:\SG, but you are given an opportunity to specify another directory or subdirectory

129

if you wish. Once the programs are installed on your hard disk, the application directory will contain the following files:

SGUI.EXE	The SDIS-GSEQ User Interface
SGUI.HLP	Help file for SGUI
SDIS.EXE	SDIS parser and converter
GSEQ.EXE	GSEQ command file parsing program
GSEQS.EXE	GSEQ pre-processing program
GSEQA.EXE	GSEQ data analysis program
PLOT.EXE	Utility program for plotting MDS files
README	This text file (called LEAME if you installed the Spanish version), contains additional information. To browse it, type README (or LEAME) at the DOS prompt (or use any word processor).
README.BAT	Batch file for browsing README
BROWSER.COM	File browser

In addition, example data files are installed in a subdirectory called EXAMPLES.

The README (or LEAME) file contains information about disk contents and installation, about running SDIS and GSEQ from a command line; a listing of SDIS error messages as well as GSEQ error, warning, and information messages; a listing of critical disk error messages; detailed Stats command options; detailed Window command specifications; information about the PLOT program; and information about the Spanish version, including command translations.

To install all files, a minimum of 600 kbytes of disk space is needed. Moreover, when SDIS and GSEQ are running, they usually save temporary files, which are automatically deleted when the programs terminate normally. Their sizes depend on the actual data being analyzed, but for most analyses 1,000 kbytes (about 1 Mbyte) of free disk space will suffice. If your data file contains many different codes, many sessions or subjects, and long sequences, then you will probably need more than 1 Mbyte of disk space for the temporary files. Note also that MDS and OUT files (which are created by SDIS and GSEQ and remain on the disk) may also be very large. A minimum of 2 Mbytes of free disk space (after installation) is recommended. If the programs terminate abnormally, temporary files (with extension $$$) remain on the disk; however, they are deleted automatically the next time the programs are invoked.

Table A.1. *SDIS running options.*

Opt	Action	Default
-e	Do not echo to screen	Echo
-s	Create summary file (INF)	None
-d	Do not create definition file (DEF)	Create
-m	Do not create modified SDIS file (MDS)	Create
-i	Disable case sensitivity	Enable
-x	Disable code exclusivity checking	Enable
-n	Enable repeated codes checking	Disable
-p	Display all nonfatal errors	Only first 30

Note: Option -m activates option -d as well. Remember, if you plan to use GSEQ, then DEF and MDS files are required.

A.2 Running the programs

The programs run in MS-DOS 3.0 or higher. SDIS and GSEQ may be invoked either from the DOS command line or from SGUI. See chapter 9 for information on running the programs from the interface.

Running SDIS

To invoke SDIS from the DOS command line, type one of the following:

SDIS or SDIS ?	Brief help information is displayed.
SDIS *filename*	Program SDIS processes data file *filename* using default options. If no extension is provided, SDS is assumed.
SDIS *fn* {-*options*}	Several options may follow the filename. Options are entered as letters preceded by a hyphen.

SDIS running options, which reverse program defaults, are given in Table A.1.

Running GSEQ

To invoke GSEQ from the DOS command line, type one of the following:

Table A.2. *GSEQ running options.*

Opt	Action	Default
-e	Do not echo to screen	Echo
-s	Make semicolons optional	Required
-v	Suppress output verbosity	Verbose
-n	Suppress output pagination	Pagination
-o	Overwrite output file	Append
-x	Print results using 133 columns	80 columns
-a	Use extended ASCII characters for display	Normal ASCII
-t	Do not print header	Print header

Note: When invoked from SGUI, SDIS and GSEQ options are menu driven. GSEQ option -t cannot be selected from SGUI.

GSEQ or GSEQ ?   Brief help information is displayed.
GSEQ *filename*   Program GSEQ processes data file *filename* using default options. If no extension is provided, GSQ is assumed.
GSEQ *fn* {*-options*}   Several options may follow the filename. Options are entered as letters preceded by a hyphen.

GSEQ running options, which reverse program defaults, are given in Table A.2.

Running SGUI

To run SGUI, type one of the following:

SGUI ?   Brief help information is displayed.
SGUI   Program starts at the main menu.
SGUI *filename*   If *filename* has extension .GSQ, then SGUI calls GSEQ for analyzing the file as a GSEQ command file. If no extension is provided, extension .GSQ is assumed. If *filename* has extension .SDS, then SGUI call SDIS for processing the file as an SDIS data file. In both cases, once the file has been processed control is returned to the SGUI main menu.

Table A.3. *Files used by SDIS and GSEQ.*

Files	Created by	Name	Extension
SDIS files	User	Any	SDS
Modified SDIS files	SDIS	Same as SDS file	MDS
	GSEQ (SAVE)	Any	MDS
Definition files	SDIS	Same as SDS file	DEF
	GSEQ (SAVE)	Same as MDS file	DEF
Summary files	SDIS	Same as SDS file	INF
GSEQ command files	User	Any	GSQ
GSEQ output files	GSEQ	Same as GSQ file	OUT
Exported tables	GSEQ (EXPORT)	Any	DAT*
Exported SPSS files	GSEQ (EXPORT)	Any	SPS*
Exported BMDP files	GSEQ (EXPORT)	Any	INP*
Exported ILOG files	GSEQ (EXPORT)	Any	IDF

*Default extensions; other extensions may be specified if desired.

A minimum of 400 kbytes of free memory is required for running SDIS and GSEQ from SGUI. A large amount of data and/or many analysis commands can make the analysis process slow. We strongly recommended that you run SDIS-GSEQ on a 386, 486, or Pentium computer with a clock running at 33 MHz or more, preferably with a preinstalled disk-cache driver.

The SDIS-GSEQ programs are coded in Borland's Turbo C 2.0 and use Mike Smedley's CXL 5.2 extended function library.

A.3 Files used by SDIS and GSEQ

The SDIS-GSEQ programs read and save a number of files, which are identified by their extensions. Table A.3 lists these files along with relevant information about them.

B

SDIS syntax and GSEQ commands

This appendix presents a reference guide to SDIS syntax and GSEQ commands. Throughout, uppercase indicates a command, entered exactly as shown, and lowercase italic indicates a word chosen by the user (filenames, codes, variable names, and so forth). Choices enclosed in braces {*like this*} are optional. Choices enclosed in brackets [*like this*] are mandatory. A vertical line separates choices when only one may be selected. A colon separates choices when more than one may be selected. Ellipses (three dots) indicate that previous items may repeat. Any punctuation sign that is not a brace, bracket, vertical line, colon, or ellipses is a part of the syntax.

B.1 SDIS syntax

Data structure

data_type { *code_declaration* } ;
{ <*subject_label*> }
data . . . ;
data . . . ;
. . .
data . . . /
{ <*subject_label*> }
data . . . ;
. . .
data . . . { (*variable_level*, . . .) } /
{ <*subject_label*> }
data . . . ;
data . . . ;
. . .
data . . . /
{ <*subject_label*> }
data . . . ;

134

. . .
data . . . { (*variable_level*, . . .) } /
. . .

Data_type

[Event |
State |
Timed |
Interval { = *observing_interval* {.*recording_interval*} {'|"} }]

Code_declaration

code{,} *code*{,} . . .

or

({ $*set_name* = } *code*{,} *code*{,} . . .)

or a mixing of both.

Data

(1) Event sequential data

{ ,*session_onset* }
code . . .
{ ,*session_offset*{)} } ;

(2) State sequential data:

{ ,*session_onset* }
code=duration . . .
{ & }
code=duration . . .
{ & }
. . .
{ ,*session_offset*{)} } ;

or

{ ,*session_onset* }
code,onset . . .
{ & }
code,onset . . .
{ & }

. . .
{ ,*session_offset*{)} } ;

Note: Formats *code=duration* and *code,onset* may mix, if separated by an ampersand.

(3) Timed event sequential data

{ ,*session_onset* }
code,time . . .
{ & }
code,time . . .
{ & }
. . .
{ ,*session_offset*{)} } ;

where time can be one of the following:

onset	occurrence time for a standard code
onset-	onset time for a standard code
onset-offset{)}	onset and (inclusive) offset time for a standard code
+onset	onset time for a context code
-offset{)}	(inclusive) offset time for a context code

(4) Interval sequential data

{ *code* { + | [- | -)] } . . . } { **repetition* } , . . . ;

B.2 GSEQ commands

Command names longer than four letters may be abbreviated to the first four (or, in the case of LAG, to the first three), as indicated by uppercase letters in the descriptions that follow.

General commands

These commands (File, Rename, Title, Variables, Pool, and End) describe the data, specify how to pool the results, or simply signal the end of GSEQ commands.

FILE *"filename"* { NOCAse : REPChk : NOEXcl } ;

declares the name of the data file to be analyzed and begins a block of commands (called a file block) that ends with the end of the command file, an explicit END command, or another File command. *Filename* follows DOS conventions. The default path is the current directory. If no extension is given, or if it is MDS, GSEQ assumes that *filename* is a modified SDIS file that has already been processed by SDIS and that the corresponding DEF file is in the same directory. If SDS or any extension other than MDS is given, GSEQ assumes that *filename* is an SDIS file not yet processed by SDIS. In that case, GSEQ calls SDIS to check the syntax and, if correct, creates the corresponding MDS and DEF files. Specify NOCASE if: (1) *filename* is an SDIS file and you want SDIS called with the Case Sensitivity option set to *no*; (2) *filename* is an MDS file created with Case Sensitivity set to *no* and you want case ignored for codes in the GSEQ command file (specifying NOCASE when the MDS file was created with Case Sensitivity set to *yes* is an error). Once NOCASE is specified, GSEQ ignores case for all codes in the current file block. Specify REPCHK if *filename* is an SDIS file and you want SDIS called with the Repeated code check option set to *yes*. Specify NOEXCL if *filename* is an SDIS file and you want SDIS called with the Exclusivity check option set to *no*.

RENAme *new_code = old_code* . . . ;

assigns new names to codes that were used in the data file. If used, RENAME must follow the FILE command. Only one RENAME command may be specified. Once a code is assigned a new name, the old name can no longer be used in the current FILE block. New names may have up to 16 characters (although we recommend using no more than 7, the number usually displayed by GSEQ), and must follow SDIS conventions. The maximum number of old codes is 95; any number of them may be renamed.

TITLe *"title"* ;

prints *title* at the beginning of every page of the output file. Its length is limited to 80 characters.

[VARIables | VARS] *variable_name = variable_number*
(*condition_name = condition_number* . . .) . . . ;

assigns names to design variables and their conditions, if any. If used, VARIABLES must follow FILE (if no RENAME command is requested) or RENAME. Only one VARIABLE command may be specified. Variable names and condition names may have up to 16 characters and must follow SDIS conventions regarding names. Variable numbers are the positions corresponding to the variables in the SDIS condition specifications. Condition numbers are the numbers enclosed within parentheses in the SDIS condition specifications. Not all the variables and conditions need to be assigned names. However, you must assign names to any variables used in subsequent POOL commands.

POOL [+|NO+ : *|NO* : *variable_name* . . .] ;

specifies the pooling of data over sessions, subjects, and variables. A plus sign means pool over sessions. An asterisk means pool over subjects. To pool over a variable, include its name (as given on a previous VARS command); otherwise results are printed separately for each level of the variable. The default is:

POOL + NO* ;

that is, pool over sessions within subjects but do not pool over subjects or variables, if any. Specifications on any POOL command remain in effect until a new POOL command is encountered in the command file.

END { ; }

stops processing of the GSEQ command file. Any other commands following the END command are ignored by GSEQ. The END command is optional. If used, it must follow either Target, Lag, Given, Simple, Save, or Export.

Data modification commands

Data modification commands (Recode, Lump, Chain, Remove, And, Or, Not, Nor, Xor, Event, Window, and Save) are used to perform data modifications or save modified data. Data modifications remain in effect until an end of file, an END command, or a new FILE command is encountered in the GSEQ command file. The effect of data modifications is cumulative. The initial data file on disk remains unaltered. The modifications are temporary (i.e., are in effect for this run only) unless saved to a disk file with the SAVE command.

RECOde *new_code = old_code1 old_code2 . . .* ;

assigns a single name to several codes defined in the data file so that every occurrence of any of the old codes is treated as an occurrence of the new code. The number of old codes is limited to 20. After RECOding, old codes become undefined, thus any reference to them in subsequent commands is an error. RECODE may be used with any data type.

LUMP [*new_code = old_code1 old_code2 . . .* | *] ;

assigns a single name (if codes are named on the command) to several codes defined in the data file so that every occurrence of any of the old codes is treated as an occurrence of the new code; in addition, sequences of old codes are treated as single occurrences of the new code. The number of old codes is limited to 20. After LUMPing, old codes become undefined, thus any reference to them in subsequent commands is an error. If no codes are named, but an asterisk is specified instead, then any consecutive repetitions of existing codes are eliminated (in this case, no new codes are created). LUMP may be used with any data type except ISD.

CHAIn *new_code = old_code1 old_code2 . . .* ;

assigns a single name to a sequence of old codes defined in the data file so that every occurrence of the sequence is treated as an occurrence of the new code. Unlike other data modification commands, the order in which the old codes are specified is important, and a code may appear more than once after the equals sign. The maximum sequence length is 20. Codes appearing after the equals sign remain defined and so may be referenced in subsequent commands. CHAIN may be used with ESD and ISD.

REMOve *old_code1 old_code2 . . .* ;

removes the old codes from consideration (i.e., makes them undefined). The number of old codes is limited to 20. REMOVE may be used with any data type.

AND *new_code = old_code1 old_code2 . . .* ;

assigns a new code to every time unit in which all the old codes co-occur. The number of old codes is limited to 20. Old codes remain defined and so may be referenced in subsequent commands. AND may be used with multiple stream SSD, TSD, and ISD.

OR *new_code = old_code1 old_code2 . . .* ;

assigns a new code to every time unit in which at least one of the old codes occurs. The number of old codes is limited to 20. Old codes remain defined and so may be referenced in subsequent commands. OR may be used with multiple stream SSD, TSD, and ISD.

NOT *new_code = old_code1 old_code2 . . .* ;

assigns a new code to every time unit in which all the old codes do not co-occur (some but not all may co-occur); NOT is the negation of AND. The number of old codes is limited to 20. Old codes remain defined and so may be referenced in subsequent commands. NOT may be used with multiple stream SSD, TSD, and ISD.

NOR *new_code = old_code1 old_code2 . . .* ;

assigns a new code to every time unit in which none of the old codes occur. NOR is the negation of OR. The number of old codes is limited to 20. Old codes remain defined and so may be referenced in subsequent commands. OR may be used with multiple stream SSD, TSD, and ISD.

XOR *new_code = old_code1 old_code2 . . .* ;

assigns a new code to every time unit in which one and only one of the old codes occurs. XOR is the exclusive OR. The number of old codes is limited to 20. Old codes remain defined and so may be referenced in subsequent commands. XOR may be used with multiple stream SSD, TSD, and ISD.

EVENt ;

ignores any time information; thus data are regarded as if they were ESD. EVENT may be used with SSD and TSD. Codes with concurrent onsets are considered as concurrent events.

WINDow *new_code* = *time_period* ;

defines a time period anchored with reference to onsets and/or offsets of an existing code. One syntax for time periods is:

[*code* | (*code* | *code*)] { +*n* | -*n* }

where *n* is an integer greater than 0 but not more than 100. This designates a time period that includes all time units or intervals for which the code is indicated, or only the onset or offset time unit or interval as noted by a left parenthesis before or a right parenthesis after the code, respectively. A plus or minus sign extends the period forward or backward *n* time units or intervals, respectively. A second syntax for time periods is:

[code | (code | code)] { +n | -n } , [code | (code | code)]
    { +m | -m }

where *n* and *m* are integers greater than 0 but not more than 100. Here the onset for the time period is the onset for the specification before the comma and the offset for the time period is the offset for the specification after the comma. If the onset occurs after the offset, an error results. WINDOW may be used with SSD, TSD, and ISD.

SAVE "*filename*" { OVERwrite } ;

saves the previous data modifications to a new MDS file (the corresponding DEF file is also created). The file includes the original data along with any modifications, and may be referenced by a subsequent FILE command. *Filename* follows DOS conventions; an extension is not required (GSEQ automatically uses MDS). Specify OVERWRITE if *filename*.MDS and *filename*.DEF already exist and you want them replaced. If they exist, and you fail to specify OVERWRITE, the modifications are not saved. SAVE must follow a data modification command; it could be the last command in the file or it could precede the END command or a FILE command beginning another block of commands.

Number of codes after modification

As a result of using data modification commands the total number of codes may change. These changes are detailed in Table B.1.

Table commands

Table commands (Target, Lag, Given, Stats, Zeros, Simple, and Export) are used to specify two-dimensional tables of tallies, request particular statistics, and export data.

Table B.1. *Results of using data modification commands.*

Command	Are old codes now undefined?	Can number of streams increase?	Number of codes after modification
RECODE	Yes	No	$n - m + 1$
LUMP	Yes	No	$n - m + 1$
LUMP*	–	No	n
CHAIN	No	Yes	$n + 1$
REMOVE	Yes	No	$n - m$
AND to XOR	No	Yes	$n + 1$
EVENT	–	No	n
WINDOW	No	Yes	$n + 1$

Note: n is the number of codes before data modification, and m is the number of different existing codes named on REMOVE or after the equals sign for the other commands.

TARGet [*code* . . . | * | *$set_name*] { & } ;

defines the target codes or column categories of a two-dimensional table of tallies. You may specify either an explicit list of codes, an asterisk, or a set name. No more than 20 explicit codes may be listed; initial codes and new ones created with data modification commands may be used. An asterisk indicates all codes currently defined, which includes all codes in the original file and any new ones created with data modifications, but excludes any that became undefined as a result of a data modification command. A set name preceded by a dollar sign indicates the set of codes declared in the initial SDIS data file. If you specify an asterisk or a set name, codes are ordered according to their order of declaration. If you specify an asterisk or a set name that implies more than 20 codes, GSEQ will truncate the code list to 20. In any event, the code list is hierarchical (codes occurring earlier in the list have preference when tallied) in order to ensure mutual exclusivity. Appending an ampersand (the residual code) to the explicit or implicit code list adds a column to the table and insures that the code list is exhaustive. TARGET may be the last command in the file, precede the END command, or precede a FILE command beginning another block of commands.

LAGs *lag* { *lag* . . . } { TO *lag* } ;

tallies lag frequencies for different lags. Lags may be any integer from -100 to +100 (for positive lags, the plus sign is optional). If no lag is specified (i.e., the LAG command is not used), lag 0 frequencies are tallied. If used, LAG must follow immediately after a TARGET command. The maximum number of lags is limited to 20, either stated explicitly or implicitly by means of the word TO. LAG may be the last command in the file, precede the END command, or precede a FILE command beginning another block of commands.

> GIVEn [*code* . . . | * | $*set_name*] { & } ;

defines the given codes or row categories of a two-dimensional table of tallies. Codes may be specified explicitly or implicitly, as in the TARGET command, and an ampersand sign may be appended to the list to ensure exhaustiveness. If the GIVEN command is not used, then the given codes are assumed to be the same as those on the TARGET command. If used, the GIVEN command must follow immediately after either a TARGET or LAG command. GIVEN may be the last command in the file, precede the END command, or precede a FILE command beginning another block of commands.

> STATs [ALL | {JNTF|NOJF} : EXPF : RSDL : ADJR : CONP
> : XSQ : GSQ : KAPPa : ODDS : YULQ]
> { (TEST | MREP | NREP | NRCK) } ;

computes and displays statistics for the two-dimensional tables specified by TARGET, LAG, and GIVEN commands, and also specifies computational options for lagged statistics when codes cannot follow themselves. The statistics you can specify are

JNTF	Observed joint or lag frequencies
EXPF	Expected frequencies under the null hypothesis
RSDL	Raw residuals (JNTF – EXPF)
ADJR	Adjusted residuals
CONP	Estimates of conditional probabilities
XSQ	Pearson's chi-square statistic
GSQ	Fisher's maximum-likelihood chi-square statistic
KAPPa	Cohen's kappa (for square tables)
ODDS	Odds ratio (for 2×2 tables)
YULQ	Yule's Q (for 2×2 tables)

If you do not include a STATS command, JNTF is printed by default. If you do not want joint frequencies, specify NOJF. If you request EXPF, or any other statistic that uses them, they are computed as described in chapter 8, depending on whether the SDIS repeat code check was set to *no* (the default) or *yes* when the MDS file was created. If you want to override the default, indicate the desired option within parentheses before the terminating semicolon. These options are

MREP   Even if the repeat code check option was *yes*, compute all expected frequencies at all lags using MM (equation (8.4)); no transitions are regarded as structurally zero.

NREP   Even if the repeat code check option was *no* (and assuming ESD and the same codes on both target and given lists), at lag 1 absolute regard all autotransitions as structurally zero and compute expected frequencies with IPF. At lags greater than 1 absolute compute expected frequencies using GS (equation (8.23)).

NRCK   Even if the repeat code check option was *no* (and assuming ESD and the same codes on both target and given lists), at lag 1 absolute regard all autotransitions as structurally zero and compute expected frequencies with IPF. At lags greater than 1 absolute compute expected frequencies using CK (equation (8.24)).

TEST   If the repeat code check option was *yes*, proceed as if NREP had been specified. If the repeat code check option was *no*, proceed as if MREP had been specified. TEST is the default.

The Stats command must precede (not follow) the Target and Given commands to which it applies, and it then applies to all tables produced thereafter by subsequent Target commands until another Stats command (if any) is encountered. If an additional Stats command is encountered, defaults are reset and the new specifications replace the old ones.

ZEROs { (} *row1* { , } *col1* {) } { { , } { (} *row2* { , } *col2* {) } ... } ;

computes expected frequencies using the Iterative Proportional Fitting algorithm at lag 1 (positive) and treats the specified cells as structural zeros, no matter what they contain and no matter the data type and the codes included in the target and given lists. Cells are identified by their row and column numbers, which must be greater than 0 but no greater than 20. Commas may be used to separate cell indexes, and each pair of indexes may be enclosed within parentheses. The maximum number of pairs is limited to 20. If used, this command must follow immediately after a STATS command. If no EXPF, RSDL, ADJR, XSQ, or GSQ were requested in the STATS command, ZEROS has no effect. No matter which options, if any, were requested in the STATS command, ZEROS overrides them at lag 1.

SIMPle [ALL I FREQ : RELF : RATE { *factor} : DURA :
RELD : PROB : AVGD] { (code ...) } ;

computes and displays descriptive or simple statistics. The statistics you can specify are

FREQ   Frequencies
RELF   Relative frequencies (FREQ / sum of FREQs)
RATE   Rates (FREQ / total session duration)
DURA   Durations
RELD   Relative durations (DURA / sum of DURAs)
PROB   Probabilities (DURA / total session duration)
AVGD   Average durations (DURA / FREQ)

Specify ALL for all the permitted statistics given the data type. In ISD, estimates of durations according to Suen and Ary's (1989) post-hoc corrections are also printed if DURA is requested. By default, statistics for all the codes currently defined are printed. If you want statistics for some codes only, specify them within parentheses before the terminating semicolon. By default, RATE is computed per 60 time units; you may choose another factor for computing rates. SIMPLE may be the last command in the command file, precede the END command, or precede a FILE command beginning another block of commands.

EXPOrt "filename" { SPSSx I BMDP I ILOG } { OVERwrite } ;

saves tables of lag frequencies (that have been previously requested by means of TARGET/LAG/GIVEN commands) to an external ASCII file. The number of tables saved depends on the current POOL specifications and the number of different lags requested. Cell indexes and tallies are saved. *Filename* follows DOS conventions; an extension is not required. The formatting options are

SPSSx   Tables saved are preceded by SPSSX or BMDP
BMDP   commands defining variables, labels, etc. If
         filename has no extension, GSEQ uses extensions
         SPS or INP, respectively.

Table B.2. *Restrictions on the order of GSEQ commands.*

Command	Follows	Precedes
File	–	G, Rename, Vars
Rename	File	G, Vars
Title*	Any command	G
Vars	File, Rename	G
Pool*	Any command	G
End	Save, Target, Lag, Given, Simple, Export	–
Recode*	Any command	G, Save
Lump*	Any command	G, Save
Chain*	Any command	G, Save
Remove*	Any command	G, Save
And*	Any command	G, Save
Or*	Any command	G, Save
Not*	Any command	G, Save
Nor*	Any command	G, Save
Xor*	Any command	G, Save
Event*	Any command	G, Save
Window*	Any command	G, Save
Save	Recode through Window	G, File, End
Target*	Any command	G, File, Lag, Given, Export, End
Lag	Target	G, File, Given, Export, End
Given	Target, Lag	G, File, Export, End
Stats*	Any command	G, Zeros
Zeros	Stats	G
Simple*	Any command	G, File, End
Export	Target, Lag, Given	G, File, End

Note: G indicates any G set command; these commands are identified with an asterisk. All commands are optional except FILE. However, every GSEQ command file must include at least one SIMPLE or one TARGET or one SAVE command.

ILOG   Tables are saved in ILOG format, together with information about variables, labels, and so forth. GSEQ uses extension IDF, overriding any extension specified by user.

If no option is specified, GSEQ saves tables only, without any information about variables, labels, and so forth. If *filename* has no extension, GSEQ uses extension .DAT. Specify OVERWRITE if *filename* already exists and you want it replaced. If it exists, and you do not specify

OVERWRITE, the tables are not saved. EXPORT can be requested only immediately after TARGET (if no LAG or GIVEN commands are specified), or after LAG (if no GIVEN command is specified), or after GIVEN. EXPORT may be the last command in the file, precede the END command, or precede a FILE command beginning another block of commands.

Order of GSEQ commands

The following commands constitute what we call the set of G commands:

> Title, Pool, Recode, Lump, Chain, Remove, And, Or, Not,
> Nor, Xor, Event, Window, Target, Stats, and Simple.

Commands that belong to this set may follow any GSEQ command, including themselves and other set members. However, GSEQ limits the number of consecutive G commands to 20 and the number of blocks of G commands after a FILE command to 20 as well. Restrictions on the order of GSEQ commands are detailed in Table B.2.

C

Critical values for chi square

df	$\alpha = .25$	$\alpha = .10$	$\alpha = .05$	$\alpha = .01$	$\alpha = .001$
1	1.323	2.71	3.84	6.63	10.83
2	2.77	4.61	5.99	9.21	13.82
3	4.11	6.25	7.81	11.34	16.27
4	5.39	7.78	9.49	13.28	18.47
5	6.63	9.24	11.07	15.09	20.5
6	7.84	10.64	12.60	16.81	22.5
7	9.04	12.02	14.07	18.48	24.3
8	10.22	13.36	15.51	20.1	26.1
9	11.39	14.68	16.92	21.7	27.9
10	12.55	15.99	18.31	23.2	29.6
11	13.70	17.28	19.68	24.7	31.3
12	14.85	18.55	21.0	26.2	32.9
13	15.98	19.81	22.4	27.7	34.5
14	17.12	21.1	23.7	29.1	36.1
15	18.25	22.3	25.0	30.6	37.7
16	19.37	23.5	26.3	32.0	39.3
17	20.5	24.8	27.6	33.4	40.8
18	21.6	26.0	28.9	34.8	42.3
19	22.7	27.2	30.1	36.2	43.8
20	23.8	28.4	31.4	37.6	45.3
21	24.9	29.6	32.7	38.9	46.8
22	26.0	30.8	33.9	40.3	48.3
23	27.1	32.0	35.2	41.6	49.7
24	28.2	33.2	36.4	43.0	51.2

df	α = .25	α = .10	α = .05	α = .01	α = .001
25	29.3	34.4	37.7	44.3	52.6
26	30.4	35.6	38.9	45.6	54.1
27	31.5	36.7	40.1	47.0	55.5
28	32.6	37.9	41.3	48.3	56.9
29	33.7	39.1	42.6	49.6	58.3
30	34.8	40.3	43.8	50.9	59.7
40	45.6	51.8	55.8	63.7	73.4
50	56.3	63.2	67.5	76.2	86.7
60	67.0	74.4	79.1	88.4	99.6
70	77.6	85.5	90.5	100.4	112.3
80	88.1	96.6	101.9	112.3	124.8
90	98.6	107.6	113.2	124.1	137.2
100	109.1	118.5	124.3	135.8	149.4

Note: Abridged from Table 8, Pearson and Hartley (1970). Adapted by permission of the *Biometrika* Trustees.

References

Adamson, L. B., & Bakeman, R. (1984). Mothers' communicative actions: Changes during infancy. *Infant Behavior and Development, 7,* 467–478.

Allison, P. D., & Liker, J. K. (1982). Analyzing sequential categorical data on dyadic interaction: A comment on Gottman. *Psychological Bulletin, 91,* 393–403.

Altmann, J. (1974). Observational study of behaviour: Sampling methods. *Behaviour, 49,* 227–267.

Arundale, R. B. (1984). SAMPLE and TEST: Two FORTRAN IV programs for analysis of discrete-state, time-varying data using first-order Markov-chain techniques. *Behavior Research Methods, Instruments, and Computers, 16,* 335–336.

Bakeman, R. (1978). Untangling streams of behavior: Sequential analyses of observation data. In G. P. Sackett (Ed.), *Observing behavior* (Vol. 2): *Data collection and analysis methods* (pp. 63–78). Baltimore: University Park Press.

Bakeman, R. (1983). Computing lag sequential statistics: The ELAG program. *Behavior Research Methods & Instrumentation, 15,* 530–535.

Bakeman, R. (1991). Counts and codes: Analyzing categorical data. In B. M. Montgomery & S. Duck (Eds.), *Studying interpersonal interaction* (pp. 255–274). New York: Guilford Publications.

Bakeman, R., & Adamson, L. B. (1984). Coordinating attention to people and objects in mother–infant and peer–infant interaction. *Child Development, 55,* 1278–1289.

Bakeman, R., Adamson, L. B., & Strisik, P. (1989). Lags and logs: Statistical approaches to interaction. In M. H. Bornstein & J. Bruner (Eds.), *Interaction in human development* (pp. 241–260). Hillsdale, NJ: Erlbaum.

Bakeman, R., Adamson, L. B., Konner, M., & Barr, R. (1990). !Kung infancy: The social context of object exploration. *Child Development, 61,* 794–809.

Bakeman, R., & Dabbs, J. M., Jr. (1976). Social interaction observed: Some approaches to the analysis of behavior streams. *Personality and Social Psychology Bulletin, 2,* 335–345.

Bakeman, R., & Dorval, B. (1989). The distinction between sampling independence and empirical independence in sequential analysis. *Behavioral Assessment, 11,* 31–37.

Bakeman, R., & Gottman, J. M. (1986). *Observing interaction: An introduction to sequential analysis.* New York: Cambridge University Press.

Bakeman, R., & Quera, V. (1992). SDIS: A sequential data interchange standard. *Behavior Research Methods, Instruments, and Computers, 24,* 554–559.

Bakeman, R., & Quera, V. (Submitted). Log-linear approaches to lag-sequential analysis when consecutive codes may and cannot repeat.

Bakeman, R., & Robinson, B. F. (1994). *Understanding log-linear analysis with ILOG: An interactive approach.* Hillsdale, NJ: Erlbaum.

Bishop, Y. M. M., Fienberg, S. R., & Holland, P. W. (1975). *Discrete multivariate analysis: Theory and practice.* Cambridge, MA: MIT Press.

Budescu, D. V. (1984). Tests of lagged dominance in sequential dyadic interaction. *Psychological Bulletin, 96,* 402–414.

Castellan, N. J., Jr. (1979). The analysis of behavior sequences. In R. B. Cairns (Ed.), *The analysis of social interactions: Methods, issues, and illustrations* (pp. 81–116). Hillsdale, NJ: Erlbaum.

Cohen, J. (1960). A coefficient of agreement for nominal scales. *Educational and Psychological Measurement, 20,* 37–46.

Cohn, J. F., & Tronick, E. Z. (1987). Mother-infant face-to-face interaction: The sequence of dyadic states at 3, 6, and 9 months. *Developmental Psychology, 23,* 68–77.

Deni, R. (1977). BASIC-PLUS programs for Sackett's lag sequential analysis. *Behavior Research Methods and Instrumentation, 9,* 383–384.

Dodd, P. W., Bakeman, R., Loeber, R., & Wilson, S. C. (1981). JOINT and SEQU: FORTRAN routines for the analysis of observational data. *Behavior Research Methods and Instrumentation, 13,* 686–687.

Faraone, S. V., & Dorfman, D. D. (1987). Lag sequential analysis: Robust statistical methods. *Psychological Bulletin, 101,* 312–323.

Fienberg, S. E. (1980). *The analysis of cross-classified categorical data* (2nd ed.). Cambridge, MA: MIT Press.

Gardner, W. (1990). CONTIME: Continuous-time analysis of parallel streams of behavior. *Multivariate Behavioral Research, 25,* 205–206.

Goodman, L. A. (1968). The analysis of cross-classified data: Independence, quasi-independence, and interactions in contingency tables with or without missing entries. *Journal of the American Statistical Association, 63,* 1091–1131.

Gottman, J. M., & Roy, A. K. (1990). *Sequential analysis: A guide for behavioral researchers.* New York: Cambridge University Press.

Haberman, S. J. (1978). *Analysis of qualitative data* (Vol. 1). New York: Academic Press.

Haberman, S. J. (1979). *Analysis of qualitative data* (Vol. 2). New York: Academic Press.

Hops, H., Willis, T. A., Weiss, R. L., & Patterson, G. R. (1972). *Marital Interaction Coding System.* Eugene: University of Oregon and Oregon Research Institute.

Iacobucci, D., & Wasserman, S. (1988). A general framework for the statistical analysis of sequential dyadic interaction data. *Psychological Bulletin, 103,* 379–390.

Kienapple, K. (1987). Micro-analytic data analysis package. *Behavior Research Methods, Instruments, and Computers, 19,* 335–337.

Konner, M. (1976). Maternal case, infant behavior and development among the !Kung. In R. B. Lee & I. DeVore (Eds.), *Kalahari hunter-gatherers* (pp. 218–245). Cambridge, MA.: Harvard University Press.

Konner, M. (1977). Infancy among the Kalahari Desert San. In P. H. Leiderman, S. R. Tulkin, and A. Rosenfeld (Eds.), *Culture and infancy* (pp. 287–327). New York: Academic Press.

Lemon, R. E., & Chatfield, C. (1971). Organization of song in cardinals. *Animal Behaviour*, *19*, 1–17.

Manne, S. L., Bakeman, R., Jacobsen, P. B., Gorfinkle, K., Bernstein, D., & Redd, W. H. (1992). Adult and child interaction during invasive medical procedures. *Health Psychology*, *4*, 241–249.

Pearson, E. S., & Hartley, H. O. (Eds.). (1970). *Biometrika tables for statisticians* (Vol. 1, 3rd ed.). New York: Cambridge University Press.

Quera, V. (1990). A generalized technique to estimate frequency and duration in time sampling. *Behavioral Assessment*, *12*, 409–424.

Quera, V., & Estany, E. (1984). ANSEC: A BASIC package for lag sequential analysis of observational data. *Behavior Research Methods, Instruments, and Computers*, *16*, 303–306.

Sackett, G. P. (1979). The lag sequential analysis of contingency and cyclicity in behavioral interaction research. In J. D. Osofsky (Ed.), *Handbook of infant development* (1st ed., pp. 623–649). New York: Wiley.

Sackett, G. P., Holm, R., Crowley, C., & Henkins, A. (1979). A FORTRAN program for lag sequential analysis of contingency and cyclicity in behavioral interaction data. *Behavior Research Methods and Instrumentation*, *11*, 366–378.

Schlundt, D. G. (1982). Two PASCAL programs for managing observational data bases and for performing multivariate information analysis and log-linear contingency table analysis of sequential and nonsequential data. *Behavior Research Methods and Instrumentation*, *14*, 351–352.

Stevenson, M. B., Ver Hoeve, J. N., Roach, M. A., & Leavitt, L. A. (1986). The beginning of conversation: Early patterns of mother-infant vocal responsiveness. *Infant Behavior and Development*, *9*, 423–440.

Suen, H. K., & Ary, D. (1989). *Analyzing quantitative behavioral data*. Hillsdale, NJ: Erlbaum.

Symons, D. K., Wright, R. D., & Moran, G. (1988). Computing lag sequential statistics on dyadic time interval data: The TLAG program. *Behavior Research Methods, Instruments, and Computers*, *20*, 343–346.

Tabachnick, B. G., & Fidell, L. S. (1989). *Using multivariate statistics* (2nd ed.). New York: Harper & Row.

Van Hooff, J. A. R. A. M. (1982). Categories and sequences of behavior: Methods of description and analysis. In K. R. Scherer & P. Ekman (Eds.), *Handbook of methods in nonverbal behavior research* (pp. 362–439). Cambridge, UK: Cambridge University Press.

Wickens, T. D. (1982). *Models for behavior: Stochastic processes in psychology*. San Francisco: Freeman.

Wickens, T. D. (1989). *Multiway contingency tables analysis for the social sciences*. Hillsdale, NJ: Erlbaum.

Yoder, P. J., & Tapp, J. T. (1990). SATS: Sequential analysis of transcripts system. *Behavior Research Methods, Instruments, and Computers*, *22*, 339–343.

Index